Routledge Revivals

Studies in Sociology

First published in 1932, *Studies in Sociology* consists of essays that fall into three groups, the first concerned with the scope and method of sociology and its relation to history and social philosophy; the second devoted to an analysis of the theory of evolution as applied to society, and to a number of problems in social psychology, such as the nature of social purpose, the place of instinct in social science, the relation between instinct and emotion, and the inheritance of mental characters; while the third group deals with the claims of Eugenics, and social classes and social mobility. This book will be of interest to students of sociology, history and philosophy.

I0121876

Studies in Sociology

Morris Ginsberg

Routledge
Taylor & Francis Group
Routledge Revivals

First published in 1932
By Methuen & Co. Ltd.

This edition first published in 2024 by Routledge
4 Park Square, Milton Park, Abingdon, Oxon, OX14 4RN
and by Routledge
605 Third Avenue, New York, NY 10017

Routledge is an imprint of the Taylor & Francis Group, an informa business

Publisher's Note
The publisher has gone to great lengths to ensure the quality of this reprint but points out that some imperfections in the original copies may be apparent.

Disclaimer
The publisher has made every effort to trace copyright holders and welcomes correspondence from those they have been unable to contact.

A Library of Congress record exists under LCCN: 33004976

ISBN: 978-1-032-76463-4 (hbk)
ISBN: 978-1-003-47856-0 (ebk)
ISBN: 978-1-032-76466-5 (pbk)

Book DOI 10.4324/9781003478560

STUDIES IN SOCIOLOGY

BY

MORRIS GINSBERG, M.A., D.Lit.

MARTIN WHITE PROFESSOR OF SOCIOLOGY IN THE UNIVERSITY OF LONDON
FELLOW OF UNIVERSITY COLLEGE, LONDON

METHUEN & CO. LTD.
36 ESSEX STREET W.C.
LONDON

First Published in 1932

PRINTED IN GREAT BRITAIN

TO

HAROLD J. LASKI

PREFACE

THESE essays, with the exception of the last, which has not hitherto been published, have all appeared in different journals during the last few years. They are concerned with questions on the borderline between social philosophy, psychology, and biology, and may, it is hoped, serve to illustrate the writer's conception of the relation between these disciplines and sociology.

I am indebted to the Editors of the *Proceedings of the Aristotelian Society*, the *Journal of Philosophical Studies*, *Economica*, the *Economic Journal*, the *Rationalist Annual*, and *Man* for leave to reprint.

M. G.

THE LONDON SCHOOL OF ECONOMICS
AND POLITICAL SCIENCE
July 1932

CONTENTS

STUDIES IN SOCIOLOGY

STUDIES IN SOCIOLOGY

I

THE SCOPE OF SOCIOLOGY

SOCIOLOGY, broadly, is the study of human interactions, their conditions and consequences. Some writers would restrict its scope to the relations arising out of acts of will, but this is an unjustifiable and unworkable limitation. For, in the first place, many socially important interactions between individuals are not consciously determined or apprehended, and, in the second place, it is one of the most interesting problems confronting the student of society to determine the respective rôles of reason or rational purpose and of impulse and the unconscious in social life.

Sociology, then, should deal with the whole tissue or web of social relationships. Since these relationships, presumably, depend upon the nature of individuals in their relations (i) to one another, (ii) to the community, (iii) to the outer environment, the ideal of sociological explanation would be attained if every social event could be traced back to its sources in the vital and psychical forces of individuals as moulded by the complex interactions which constitute the life of the community, in contact with the outer environment.

But this ideal, if generously conceived, is clearly too ambitious. The relations between human beings are infinitely delicate and varied. They are hardly likely to lend themselves to scientific treatment without a great deal of preliminary classification, and it may even prove for ever impossible to exhibit precisely the way in which the life of each individual is interwoven with the lives of others in society. Some delimitation is thus clearly necessary. How is this to be achieved ?

We may, to begin with, abandon the attempt to deal with all the complex interactions of social life and confine our study to those phenomena which are widely shared by members of a community, such as language, morality, religion, or more generally, to such relations as have been embodied in recognized forms or institutions. Such institutions, it will be seen, are not themselves relations between social beings, but rather forms or modes of relationships, ultimately derived from the nature of individuals in interaction, and in turn moulding and determining further interaction. From this point of view sociology can be defined as the science of social institutions (in the broadest sense of that term), or as the science dealing with the *forms or modes* of social relationships as they are exhibited in the civilization or culture of a people, understanding by culture, with Tylor, ' that complex whole which includes knowledge, belief, art, morals, law, custom, and any other capabilities and habits acquired by man as a member of society '.

But here our difficulties begin over again. The various elements of culture have all been made the objects of study by special social sciences, for example comparative philology, ethics, jurisprudence, aesthetics, politics, economics, comparative religion. Where is the need for another social science ?

There appear to be two ways of dealing with this problem, neither unfortunately free from difficulties. It may, in the first place, be held (as by Simmel)[1] that a distinction must be drawn between the form of social relationships and their content or matter. Thus, for example, the relation of sub- and super-ordination can

[1] cf. his *Soziologie*.

be studied alike in the Church and State, in the family, or any other association. Similarly the relation of competition can be investigated in the field of economics, politics, the history of art or religion. We must single out the ultimate modes of relationship between human beings and study them as such in abstraction from the differing contents within which they are manifested. On this view the difference between sociology and the special sciences is not to be found in the nature of the particular sphere of social life with which they each deal. Such a basis of classification can only lead to the view of sociology as at best a summary of special studies such as those dealing with political organization, church organization, education and the like—an *omnium gatherum*—without any real principle or system. The difference rather is that sociology deals with the topics of all these sciences from a particular point of view, namely that of the nature of the social relationships exhibited in them, for example competition, subordination, hierarchy, forms of the maintenance of order, types of organization, etc., in short, all forms of interaction which constitute social life, or rather which appear in all spheres of social life. Sociology, then, differs from the special sciences not in being more comprehensive, but rather in dealing with the same topics from a special aspect, viz. the aspect which makes them social phenomena, or modes or forms of social life.

The distinction thus drawn is no doubt legitimate, but in practice it is exposed to all the dangers familiar in philosophical speculation whenever a distinction has been made between form and matter. The separation tends to be made too sharply, as for example when some formal logicians have thought that it is possible in Logic to abstract entirely from the matter of thought or from what one is thinking about and still find general principles or forms in accordance with which all thought whatsoever takes place. Critics of this school of logic have pointed out that this is strictly an impracticable task since the form of thought is modified according to the matter in which it appears. Attention to forms to the exclusion of matter is apt to lead to bare and empty generalities. The tendency to excessive formalization is already to be detected in some of the members of this school of sociology, some of whom have drawn up possible lists of human relationships not based upon inductive comparison and generalization, but on arm-chair philosophizing. Apart from these general difficulties, moreover, this view of sociology is open to two others. In the first place, it may easily come to regard certain forms of social relationship as involved in the nature of society or association as such, whereas in truth they may be the result of special causes, historical and psychological, or arise out of specific human interests. Whether this be so or not, it is impossible to decide without attention to the matter or content of the relationship in the different forms in which it appears. Are the poor, for example, to be always with us ? Do they arise necessarily out of the formal relation between individuals, or are they the result of special causes historically determined ?

In the second place, confusion may arise from a tendency too readily to assume that what appears to be the same relationship appearing in different contexts is due to identical causes. For example, there is a relation of subordination in the family, in the trade union, and the various forms of the State, but the nature of the subordination may be really quite different in the different cases and be due to quite different causes, psychological and other. Here again the question cannot be solved by a study of the purely formal character of the relation of subordination without giving attention to the members between whom the relationship holds in the different cases.

In mitigation of these difficulties, however, the analogy of logic may be appealed to. It may be granted in the case of this latter science that the forms of thought cannot be effectively studied apart from the particular sort of matter about which we think, yet logic is undoubtedly formal in the sense that it is not interested in the variety of the things we think about for their own sake, but only for the sake of discovering the forms involved in our thinking of them. So in sociology, it may be held that though the forms of social relationship cannot profitably be studied in complete abstraction from their contents, yet the sociologist is only interested in the latter for the sake of the light they throw upon the nature of society as such. That is the sum of social relationships. If the classification of social relationships is carried out inductively, and their conditions and consequences in each case carefully studied, it is urged this method of sociological inquiry should lead to fruitful results. So far, however, very little has been done in this direction.

The other and the more generally accepted way of delimiting the sphere of sociology in relation to the special social sciences is by reference not to form but to content. Human activities can be marked out in certain series which possess relative independence and which can be conveniently and fruitfully studied apart from their relations to other activities and functions. Thus, for example, there arise the special sciences of economics, politics, jurisprudence, pedagogics and the like, each of which is concerned with some special aspect or function of social life. A study of these special sciences shows that they have almost invariably tended to pass beyond their proper boundaries into the field of wider social activities. The reason for this is easy to see. Social activities are parts of an organic whole, and it is impossible either in theory or practice to understand the condition of a society in any one respect without taking into consideration its condition in all other respects. Moreover, social functions overlap and are difficult to classify. Thus, for example, economic satisfactions cannot be sharply divided off from non-economic satisfactions, and therefore the boundaries of economics must be more or less indefinite. For purposes of scientific investigation, however, suitable lines of demarcation are found, as, for example, when Pigou defines economics as the science which deals with that part of social welfare that can be brought directly or indirectly into relation with the measuring rod of money. Strictly the causal propositions laying down the conditions upon which economic welfare depends must be regarded as claiming to be true subject to the condition that things outside the economic sphere remain constant. It is undoubtedly of the greatest importance from the point of view of scientific method to make the abstractions thus rendered necessary and the history of science shows that progress depends largely upon such analytic procedure. Similar remarks apply to other special social sciences. But it is equally important to recognize that each of these sciences *is* abstract in character, and that the conclusions of each must be corrected so as to make allowance for interfering factors which fall outside its own special field of study. Again, to take the case of economics once more, the conditions which determine economic welfare are to a great extent influenced by the general state of society at any given time, and in turn react upon social life as a whole. In relation to economics we may therefore say there is need for a wider social science which will (i) correct the abstractions it necessarily makes in the light of knowledge derived from other social sciences, (ii) consider the effects of economic processes upon the wider social life, (iii) consider the influence of social life and structure as a whole upon economic conditions. *Mutatis mutandis* this may be said also of the other special social sciences, and thus we arrive at a general description of sociology as the science which deals with social life as a whole in contra-distinction from the special sciences which deal with special aspects of human life. More clearly perhaps we may say that sociology (i) deals with the broader conditions of social life which because of their generality do not come within the scope of the special social sciences, and (ii) brings together the results of the specialisms making the adjustments which are required, in view of the fact that the parts of the social life with which they severally deal are of varying importance in determining the life of society viewed as a whole.

There are thus two divergent ways of interpreting the relation between sociology and the special social sciences. The one, exemplified by Simmel and his followers, would regard sociology as a specialism among other specialisms whose object is to discover the ultimate forms of social relationships as such, while the other regards sociology as an attempt at a synthetic view of the social life utilizing the results of the various social sciences, but interpreting them in the light of the broader principles of social organization which often escape the specialist. The former school do not, it seems to me, sufficiently realize that in a sense all sciences are formal, in the sense, namely, that each deals with what is common to different individuals, or with the general forms exemplified in different materials. The distinction between form and matter must in other words be made within each of the special sciences, and the difference between them and sociology should be expressed by saying that while the former deal with special forms, the latter deals with more general forms. Now in each of the social sciences, if developed along realistic lines, it is extremely difficult, as we have seen, to separate form from matter at all clearly. This is due to the extreme complexity of the relations with which they deal. In economics, for instance, 'we are in the position in which the physicist would be if tin attracted iron in the inverse ratio of the cube of its distance, lead in that of the square of its distance, and copper in some other ratio. We cannot say, as he can of his attractions, that the amount offered or required of every several commodity is one and the same specified function of the price. All that we can say in this general way is that it is some one of a specified large family of functions of the price. Hence in Economics there is not, as in Dynamics, one fundamental law of general application, but a great number of laws, all expressible, as it were, in equations of similar form, but with different constants'.[1] Similar remarks apply to other social sciences. It is clear that even in these sciences the matter affects the form to a degree which makes their undue separation extremely dangerous. This danger must surely be enhanced as we ascend in generality and abstraction towards sociology conceived as a special science of forms of social relationships. I doubt, therefore, whether sociology in this sense can ever be an independent science. It may have use as one method among others, but its conclusions will always have to be tested by appeal to the concrete facts of social life, and this surely necessitates a sociology in the second sense, which seeks to interpret social life as a concrete whole.[2]

[1] Pigou, *Economics of Welfare*, p. 9.

[2] In a recent work, *The Science and Method of Politics* (Kegan, Paul, 1927, pp. xii + 360, 12*s*. 6*d*.), Dr. Catlin defines Politics as the science which deals with 'the relations of individuals to each other in society, regarded in respect of the relationship itself'. This corresponds pretty closely to the view of sociology here criticized. Leaving aside the verbal question as to whether this general science should be called Politics or Sociology, we may note that Dr. Catlin's view seems exposed to the difficulties raised above in reference to sociology and to two others peculiar to his

I shall return later to the question of the nature and possibilities of such a comprehensive interpretation. Meanwhile attention must be drawn to certain topics of investigation which by general consent fall within the scope of sociology. These include the various forms of social grouping, such as crowds, sects, social classes, tribes, clans, nations, races and the large variety of institutions and the modes and methods of organization by which they are maintained and developed. It is true that in the study of these, many specialisms have developed, such as, for example, ethnology, which deals with the physical and mental characters of races, their origin and distribution, or political science, which, in one of its aspects, deals with forms of governmental administration. But these fall within the sociological field and may be regarded as specialisms within it.[3] The importance of the study of the nature and conditions of social groupings is surely obvious. It is, for example, of enormous consequence to discover under what conditions the social entity we call a 'nation' arises. Yet very few really scientific studies of this question have so far been made, though there are signs that the need for inductive studies on a large scale is being gradually recognized.[4] Similarly social classes both admit of and require study on the basis of wide inductive and comparative surveys. Here again only beginnings have as yet

own method of treatment. He intensifies the abstract character of the inquiry, in the first place, by limiting his analysis to one type of social relationship, namely, that which arises out of the domination of one will by another, and in the second place, by proceeding on the assumption that this one type of relationship is determined by a single motive, the will to power, or, more accurately, the striving to avoid or assert control. Such very abstract procedure can hardly conduce to fruitful results in social inquiry.

[3] Similarly anthropology on its cultural and social side may be described as the sociology of the simpler peoples.

[4] cf. S. R. Steinmetz, *Die Nationalitäten in Europa*, 1927.

been made.[1] In other spheres of social life greater progress has been achieved, as, for example, in the comprehensive studies made by Prof. Westermarck on marriage and the family.[2]

But while the importance of the comparative study of social institutions will be admitted by most students of society, yet many will doubt whether the time has yet arrived for the scientific study of the inter-relations between them and for the formulation of theories regarding the nature of society as a whole. As to these doubts, which the facile generalizations and extravagant claims made by some sociologists justly provoke, several things have to be said. In the first place, the special scientist does not, and can not, really abandon the problem of the inter-relations referred to above. The realistically inclined economist, for example, must take into consideration the relations both in the way of cause and effect between economic factors and such things as the class spirit, national sentiment, race prejudice, the general position of women and the like, but there being no body of systematic doctrine on these matters, his procedure is frequently amateurish and unbalanced. Another illustration may be given from the history of science, which is much in need of sociological treatment. The specialist is rarely in the position to estimate fairly the relation between the growth of his own science and branches of thought rather remote from his training and experience, and still less between it and the wider aspects of social life. But generalizations on these subjects are extremely common, while the evidence upon which they rest is generally slight and often not given at all. Is there not therefore a good case for the necessity of a

[1] cf. especially Fahlbeck, *Die Klassen und die Gesellschaft*, 1922.

[2] On the sociology of religion reference may be made to the works of Max Weber, Troeltsch, and Tawney.

systematic treatment of the sociological conditions of science and conversely of the effects of science upon the life of communities ? [1]

At this point the opponent of sociology may urge that while he is prepared to admit the importance of the study of social institutions in given areas or periods and even the desirability of intensive study of the inter-relations between them, he yet doubts the possibility of a single comprehensive science of human society as a whole claiming to formulate the general laws of its evolution or development. This attitude is now extremely common among anthropologists and historians. To some extent it is the result of a natural reaction against the too ambitious schemes of social evolution formulated, often on data inadequate both quantitatively and qualitatively, by some of the earlier sociologists. In part, also, this attitude is a form of the widely felt scepticism with regard to many aspects of the theory of biological evolution and the consequent demand to turn

[1] An extremely interesting illustration of such a sociological treatment of science is to be found in Prof. Whitehead's *Science and the Modern World* (see Chapter I : ' The Origins of Modern Science '), where he traces the various factors which throughout the Middle Ages prepared the intellect of Western Europe for the acceptance of the notion of orderliness in nature, for the belief in the scrutability of nature and for the interest in natural objects and occurrences for their own sake. Some of his views, however, need a great deal more justification than his short discussion provides. For example, he asserts that the deep-seated belief that every occurrence can be correlated with its antecedents in accordance with general principles, which dominates the minds of European scientists, has its main origin in the medieval insistence on the rationality of God, in contrast with the Asiatic view of God as either arbitrary or impersonal. Is this really warranted by the available evidence or a mere guess ? *Prima facie* one would have thought Buddhistic metaphysics more sympathetic to the notion of law in nature, and again that in Western Europe the notion of a necessary natural order is more likely to have arisen by way of reaction to that of a personal God ruling by the fiat of his will than as an unconscious and natural derivative from it.

from morphology to physiology and to abandon the study of origins in favour of the careful analysis of process and function. That there are elements of value in this sceptical movement must be conceded. It rightly insists on the need of caution in the use of anthropological data which are inevitably of very unequal evidentiary value and in the application of common categories to peoples differing widely in the scale of civilization. It is also on sound lines when it stresses the difficulties of comparing the institutions of a given area with the 'similar' institutions of other areas, on the ground that each area is a unity, having a peculiar self-identity, with the result that the nature of institutions is distorted when they are studied apart from the culture-complex to which they belong. At the same time there is a certain lack of proportion in the attacks now so frequently made upon what is called 'evolutionary' sociology. A number of rather different issues is involved which it is important to disentangle. In the first place the objection to evolutionary sociology is often interpreted as implying a condemnation of the use of the comparative method. This is due to a confusion easy enough to account for historically. The earlier sociologists in their eagerness to trace the stages or phases through which society has passed brought together data from all parts of the world and all periods of time without giving sufficient attention to the reliability of their data and without discriminating adequately between superficial similarities in cultural traits and genuine identities. The discredit brought upon these earlier schemes of social evolution as a result of the more careful and intensive analysis of recent anthropology is held, perhaps not unnaturally, to throw doubt upon the value of the comparative method in general, and upon the possibility of what may be called a social morphology. But it is important to recognize, to begin with, that the comparative method as such is not in the least committed to the theory of evolution. It is in essence nothing but an application of a general principle of methodology to vary the conditions of a phenomenon under investigation with the object of eliminating irrelevancies and the discovery of essentials. When applied to the study of social facts this involves the use of data from various periods of time and from the life of different peoples. The primary object is the attainment of a classification of cultural phenomena and the establishment of a social morphology which would facilitate the discovery of empirical generalizations and perhaps eventually of more ultimate laws. But morphological classification has, as such, nothing to do with the problem of the chronological order in which the varied types arise. It should be remembered that in general biology, too, taxonomy has nothing to do with the tracing of phylogeny, though, of course, if the taxonomic tree can be shown to coincide with the phylogenetic tree, that constitutes a striking piece of evidence in support of the theory of evolution. In sociology likewise the tracing of the line of evolution constitutes a problem additional to that of morphological classification.

It must in the next place be noted that the critics of the comparative method in sociology do not, in fact, themselves dispense with the use of it in their own work. The method used by some of the 'Diffusionists' consists in tracing combinations of similar cultural elements in different parts of the world and at different periods of time, and this cannot be done without the use of the comparative method. Again, when Dr. Goldenweiser, who makes much of the weaknesses of the comparative method, wishes to criticize Dr. Rivers's explanation of the secrecy, multiplicity, and graded character of the religious societies of Mota Island as due to culture mixture, he appeals to the religious associations of other areas, such as those of West Africa or North America, which exhibit the same combinations of traits in conditions which preclude culture mixture.[1] It seems clear that even in the intensive study of any area comparative material must not be disregarded. When it is disentangled from the wider issue of the value of the evolutionary hypothesis in sociology, the point of substance that remains in the attack on the comparative method is the need of more intensive studies of local areas and of greater caution in the tracing of similarities and differences in cultural phenonena.

We may next consider the larger problem of what has been described as the ' downfall of evolutionism '.[2] Here again several rather different issues are involved. To begin with, these and other writers seem to have made good their case against what may be described as the theory of unilinear social evolution, that is, the theory that all people have passed through a sequence of stages more or less in the same order. Detailed and more accurate data than were available to the earlier writers have proved that some of the alleged primitive stages, for example, promiscuity, were mythical and based upon nothing better than the desire to find an undifferentiated horde out of which later forms of social organization were to emerge in accordance with the requirements of evolutionary theory. In regard to many features of social life, such as forms of property, methods of reckoning descent, the development of art, material culture and religion, again, it was urged that they could not, either taken singly or in combination, be pressed into any regular scheme of chronological sequences. The singularity and complexity of cultural phenomena were

[1] See his chapter on ' Cultural Anthropology ' in *History and Prospects of the Social Sciences*, edited by H. E. Barnes (Knopf, 1927, pp. xxi + 534, 21s.).

[2] cf. Boas, *Rasse und Kultur*; Lowie, *Primitive Society*; Goldenweiser, *Early Civilization* and *Cultural Anthropology*.

shown to be incompatible with the view of uniformity in social development. The prevalence of diffusion, moreover, is fatal to the theory of a regular sequence of stages, since, obviously, by borrowing and the appropriation of alien ideas leaps can be made by any one people without passing through the intermediate stages. On the ground of these and similar arguments the downfall of evolutionism is triumphantly proclaimed. But though they dispose of unilinear evolution, can these arguments be held to be equally fatal to the whole idea of evolution in sociology? Clearly not. It should firstly be noted that the issue is misrepresented when it is put in the form of a contrast between 'diffusion' and 'evolution'. For, if by evolution is meant the theory of descent with modification from a common source, the believer in the diffusion of culture from a single centre would be the evolutionist *par excellence.* The problem of independent growth as against development from a single source is analogous to the problem of monogenesis and polygenesis in biology, and is therefore a subsidiary question within the general framework of evolution and not one between it and some other theory. Secondly, are not the critics of social evolution unreasonable in expecting to find absolute uniformity in development? Ought we not rather even on the analogy of biological evolution to expect endless variety and complexity, especially if it be remembered that in sociology we are not dealing with a single development, but with a large number of different developments, partly divergent and partly interconnected? The believer in evolution need not and does not now maintain that development is always in a single line, and he admits the great difficulty of finding criteria for comparing different civilizations. Yet he believes that on the whole there is continuity in the history of civilization, and he seeks to determine the forces which determine its growth. In tracing development the notion of stages of culture is by no means without value,[1] though it must not be interpreted chronologically and is in practice often extremely difficult to apply.[2] Thirdly, it may be remarked that many of the arguments of the 'anti-evolutionists' are relevant only as against the theory of inevitable or necessary progress. But here they are attacking a man of straw. The distinction between evolution and progress is now generally accepted and it is recognized that the problem of tracing the actual course of social development is distinct from that of its ethical valuation.

In sum, the notion of development has by no means yet lost its relevance and importance in the study of sociology, though, of course, it must not be assumed that the theory of social development must necessarily take the form familiar in biology, or that the forces operating in it are merely biological in character. Without in any way prejudging the ultimate issue we may say, then, that the object of sociology is:

1. To determine the nature or character of the various forms of social groupings and the institutions by which they are regulated and maintained, and to trace the line of their growth or development.

2. To determine, by means of the comparative method and, as far as possible, by the use of quantitative measurement, the inter-relations between institutions and the degree of correlated growth. In this connexion

[1] cf. the important article of E. Troeltsch, 'Der Aufbau der europäischen Kulturgeschichte', in Schmoller's *Jahrbuch*, Bd. XLIV, where he defends the notion of 'Universalgeschichte als Soziologie'.

[2] Reference should be made in this connexion to the work of Prof. Hobhouse, especially his *Social Development*; E. Troeltsch, *Dynamik der Geschichte nach der Geschichtsphilosophie des Positivismus*, in *Beiheft der Kantstudien*, 1919; Breysig, *Stufenbau und Gesetze der Weltgeschichte*, and *Kulturgeschichte der Neuzeit*; cf. also the works of Lamprecht and Schmoller, Vierkandt and Max Weber.

the phenomena of diffusion and contact are of the greatest importance.

3. To formulate empirical generalizations or laws of such growth.

4. To interpret these laws in the light of the more ultimate laws of life and mind.

In carrying out this ambitious programme the sociologist must of course avail himself of the results of many specialisms, both in the social field and in other fields of inquiry. His object throughout is to determine the relation of social facts to civilization as a whole, and this involves a vast amount of preliminary description, comparison, and correlating of results which cannot be achieved by the special sciences as such.

The relation between sociology and the special sciences should be clear from the above arguments. Special problems arise, however, as to its relation to biology, psychology, and philosophy which are extremely difficult and perplexing and have occasioned much controversy. To discuss them fully would require a volume. Here they can only be dealt with in outline, and, it is feared, in somewhat dogmatic fashion.

Biological factors are clearly of importance to the student of society, since the unit of society is a living organism. Great confusion has, however, resulted from the too facile application of biological categories to social facts, and, in particular, a tendency to over-emphasize the purely racial factors in social evolution or change. It has too often been forgotten that social facts are in a sense *sui generis*, or at any rate involve the operation of forces, psychological and social, which profoundly modify the effects of the purely biological forces. Provided he eschew vague analogies and the tendency to mistake the part for the whole, the biologist, none the less, may have much to contribute to a scientific sociology. At present the most profitable lines of

2

inquiry for the biological sociologist would seem to be in the following directions:

1. To determine the effect of individual innate differences in mental and physical characters upon the constitution of social groupings, such as classes, nations, and the like, and upon the working of social institutions generally.

2. To determine the converse operation of social institutions, by way of social selection and in other ways, upon the biological constitution of groups.

3. To study the effects of race or group contact and mixture upon society.

4. To ascertain and measure the intensity of the selective forces operating on man in society and the possibilities of controlling or modifying them by agencies under social control.

The relations between psychology and sociology are extremely close and intimate. It is clear that social facts, whatever else they may rest upon, imply relations between minds. Neither the relations of antagonism or opposition, nor those of co-operation and mutual effort, are intelligible apart from reference to instincts, desires, and purposes. Society is essentially a psychical structure, and to understand its nature we must know the laws of interaction between human minds. On the other hand, a great deal of general psychology is social psychology. Modern psychology has brought out clearly the important part played by intersubjective intercourse in moulding even the most elementary psychical functions, and the higher mental processes are permeated through and through by environing social factors. It is accordingly not surprising that there is considerable overlapping between the two sciences. Nevertheless the point of view of the psychologist and his ultimate object differ from those of the sociologist. The former is primarily interested in the nature of mental process, and he uses the data of social life to the extent to which they help him in describing the operations of the mind and the conditions of its development. The sociologist is interested not in mind as such, but rather in the part it plays in determining the nature and genesis of social phenomena, and he recognizes that these latter, though they have a psychological basis, cannot be understood in terms of psychology alone. A phenomenon like war, for example, cannot be accounted for in exclusively psychological terms. It depends also upon historical and geographical conditions, the further analysis of which renders necessary an appeal to the laws of the physical and biological sciences in so far as they bear upon human beings in interaction. In a sense social facts are, as the French sociologists especially emphasize, *sui generis* and must be interpreted primarily in terms of social fact. But this does not mean, as is sometimes thought, that the mental processes involved in social phenomena are supra-individual, or that sociology is concerned with a group mind differing in kind from the minds of individuals. The psychical elements involved are those of individual minds in interaction with one another, with the tradition of material and spiritual culture which they build up, and with the physical environment. In so far as society is supra-individual it is not a mind, nor a sum or resultant of minds, but a relational complex of a distinctive kind. In so far, however, as it does contain mental elements, it must be interpreted in terms of what we know of the individual mind.[1]

We may now indicate the main lines of investigation which fall within the sphere of social psychology. In general it seeks to determine the nature of the psychological conditions of social life. Thus it deals with the

[1] For a discussion of some further objections to the use of psychological explanation in sociology, see my article 'The Sociological Work of the late Dr. Rivers', in *Psyche*, July 1924.

means and methods of intersubjective intercourse, such as intuition of other persons, suggestion, imitation and sympathy, the elements in the human mind leading to co-operation and antagonism, leadership, domination and submission, the part played by impulses, ideas and rational purposes in social life, the degree to which social development is or can be controlled by rational will. In its more special aspects it deals with the psychological characteristics of social groups, such as races, nations, classes, occupations and the like, with the effects of these social formations upon the mentality of the individuals constituting them, and with the results of contact between groups. Progress in these more special aspects of social psychology is not very rapid, but there are signs that the need of inductive studies on a large scale is coming to be widely realized.

The relation between sociology and philosophy can be best approached, perhaps, by considering the way in which philosophy is related to other special sciences. In the first place, philosophy aims at providing a critical methodology for the special sciences; in other words, it seeks to disentangle the fundamental categories or principles which they employ, the assumptions, postulates, or pre-suppositions upon which they rest, and to subject them to critical scrutiny and constructive re-interpretation. In the second place, on its more constructive side, philosophy seeks to correct the abstractions which the special sciences are, from the nature of their method, compelled to make, and thus to present a more concrete or synoptic interpretation of reality, considered as a whole, or in its ultimate nature. In the third place, philosophy lays particular emphasis upon the consideration of the element of value in the universe, more particularly from the point of view of man's place in it. These three functions are clearly of the greatest importance in reference to the social sciences. They are, firstly, in need of a critical methodology or epistemology whose object it would be to criticize the categories employed by them and to inquire into the validity of their fundamental postulates. It is even arguable that the social sciences are at present in greater need of a logic than other special sciences. Secondly, in so far as the philosopher aims at a complete synthesis of all knowledge, he must of course take into consideration the results of the social sciences, especially if they ever come to be systematized by a comprehensive sociology. Indeed, these results are of special interest to him, since, as we have seen, philosophy lays special stress on the problem of man's place in the universe. Finally, perhaps the most important function of the social philosopher is to apply his criteria of value to the facts of social life and change, to inquire into the ethical validity of social and political ideals as distinguished from their sociological possibility. A complete view of society would thus imply a science of sociology dealing with the facts of social life (including the psychology and history of ideals in so far as they act as agents influencing social behaviour) and a social philosophy which would estimate their goodness or rightness in the light of ethical theory.

II

HISTORY AND SOCIOLOGY [1]

IN actual practice the relation between history and sociology is very close. The sociologist of necessity derives his material from the data furnished by anthropology and history. On his side the historian, however eager he may be to confine himself to detailed and close narration of actual fact, cannot avoid reference to problems of causation or assumptions regarding human nature or the general course of human evolution, and so is a sociologist *malgré lui*. Again, though there are still not wanting some historians, such as von Below, who deny sociology any status,[2] most writers on the theory and methodology of history have come to regard the two disciplines as *Hilfswissenschaften* to each other.[3] Closer examination, however, reveals considerable uncertainty and hesitation. This is due, firstly to widely prevalent doubts as to the scope of sociology, with regard to which it is said, not without some exaggeration, the sociologists themselves are not in agreement. It is due, secondly, to the fact that the issues raised involve reference to difficult problems in the theory of knowledge generally, in regard to which, in the present position of epistemology, agreement is hardly to be expected. In this paper I shall attempt, firstly, to define briefly the scope of sociology and discuss the bearing of my definition upon some recent representative views of the nature

[1] A paper read at the Anglo-American Conference of Historians, July 1931.

[2] George von Below, *Probleme der Wirtschaftsgeschichte*, p. 4.

[3] E. Bernheim, *Lehrbuch der historischen Methode*, p. 97.

of historical investigation; secondly, in the light of this discussion I will endeavour to re-state the fundamental points of our problem in the hope of bringing out more clearly the main issues involved.

Sociology in the broadest sense is the study of human interactions and interrelations, their conditions and consequences. In practice it soon becomes clear that if sociology were really to attempt to deal with the whole tissue of human relationships in their infinite complexity it would make but little headway. Accordingly, it confines itself by common consensus to the study of such social relationships as have been embodied or defined in recognized forms or institutions. Thus another definition of sociology is that it is the science of social institutions, that is the forms or modes of social relationships exhibited in culture, or the activities of men as members of society. Sociology is also sometimes defined as the science of society. This latter term is, then, intended to cover not merely forms of grouping but the whole tissue of human relationships in so far as it possesses any definiteness of pattern. In the further elaboration of these definitions two tendencies may be broadly distinguished. According to the formal school of Simmel and his disciples, the function of general sociology is to disentangle the fundamental forms of social relationship and to study them independently of their specific content. Such relationships as leadership and obedience, subordination and superordination, competition, division of labour, may, it is said, be traced in all societies, and can therefore be studied simply as relationships. It appears that Simmel himself in his later work came to regard this type of inquiry as only a part of general sociology. In any event, most other sociologists are impressed with the difficulty and the danger of separating form from matter, and regard sociology rather as the effort to interpret social life as a concrete whole. An examination of the work of outstanding sociologists such as Hobhouse, Westermarck, Max Weber, Sombart, Troeltsch will, I think, show that the functions of sociology may be thus stated : (i) It seeks to elaborate what may be called a social morphology or a classification of the types and forms of social relationships. (ii) It tries to determine the relations between the different aspects or factors of social life ; for example, between the economic and the political, the moral and the religious, the intellectual and the social elements. (iii) It endeavours to disentangle the fundamental conditions of social change and persistence, whether these be biological, psychological, or distinctively sociological, and to relate its empirical generalizations to the more ultimate laws of life and mind. Any one who doubts the reality of sociology may be invited to read some of these works. He will find that despite an obvious immaturity of which the sociologists themselves are quite sufficiently keenly aware, sociology may claim that its foundations have been well laid, and that a great deal has already been achieved not merely in the matter of methodology but in the work of classification and even in the study of causes.

Sociology must be distinguished from social philosophy. As I understand it, the latter is concerned essentially with two sets of problems. On its critical side it seeks to provide what may be called an epistemology of the social sciences, that is to say, an account of the methods, categories, and assumptions used in these sciences. There is, in other words, a philosophy of the social sciences, just as there is a philosophy of the physical sciences. On its more constructive side social philosophy is concerned with the problem of values, that is, with the application of ethical principles to the phenomena of social life and social evolution. Sociology, on the other hand, is not concerned with values, except in so far as beliefs relating to values may have causal efficacy in determining or influencing social change. Sociology may, in other words, deal with what may be called the natural history of morals or religion, but it is not, as such, concerned with the problem of their truth or validity. Its procedure is thus *naturwissenschaftlich*, even when it deals, as it must, with mental factors. Similarly, like other sciences, it is not as such concerned with epistemology or the ultimate validity of the categories which it employs. This also it leaves to social philosophy.

We may now turn to a consideration of the scope of history and of the views held by some representative and important writers of its relation to sociology. I take first the views of Prof. Bury, who has discussed this question in a well-known address on the 'Place of Modern History in the Perspective of Knowledge'.[1] Bury is above all anxious to defend the independence of history, the principle as he calls it, of 'history for its own sake'. He shows first of all that history cannot be regarded as subordinate to political science; for, unlike the latter, history deals not merely with the political aspects of society but with 'all its various activities, all the manifestations of its intellectual, emotional, and material life'. At this point, however, Bury recognizes that a more serious danger threatening the independence of history presents itself. If history differs from political science merely in inclusiveness, the conclusion seems difficult to resist that it is subordinate or ancillary to what pretends to be the most inclusive of the social sciences—sociology. 'Political science', it will be said, 'is a branch of social science, just as political history is part of general history; and the object of studying general history is simply and solely to collect and furnish material for sociological science.'[2] Bury thinks that

[1] *Selected Essays* (ed. Temperley), pp. 43–59. [2] Ibid., p. 44.

this question can only be resolved by an appeal to more ultimate philosophical considerations, ' by the view we entertain of the *moles et machina mundi* as a whole '. ' If human development can be entirely explained on the general lines of a system such as Saint-Simon's or Comte's or Spencer's, then I think we must conclude that the place of history, within the frame of such a system, is subordinate to sociology and anthropology. There is no separate or independent precinct in which she can preside supreme. But on an idealistic interpretation of knowledge it is otherwise. History then assumes a different meaning from that of a higher zoology, and is not merely a continuation of the process of evolution in nature. If thought is not the result but the presupposition of the process of nature, it follows that history, in which thought is the characteristic and guiding force, belongs to a different order of ideas from the kingdom of nature and demands a different interpretation.' This method of argument seems to me very unsatisfactory. In the first place, we are not, I think, entitled to assume at the outset that the guiding force of history is thought. Such a vast generalization could only be established, if at all, as a result of a study of the relation between mental development and social development. Even if such a view could be justified on purely philosophical grounds, I doubt whether it ought to be allowed to dominate historical theory or prescribe its postulates and assumptions. A philosophy of history ought, on the contrary, to stand the test of historical inquiry in relation to the results achieved by other sciences and by metaphysics. In the second place, I fail to see the relevance of Bury's argument to the special problem of the relation between sociology and history; for an idealistic interpretation of the nature of human development must affect sociology in exactly the same sense in which it affects history. His arguments, on his own showing, are only valid if sociology is regarded as a sort of 'higher zoology'. But for such a restriction of the nature of sociology there appears to be no ground whatever. The problem of the relation between history and sociology thus remains completely unresolved.

A more ambitious attempt to subordinate sociology to history is made by M. Berr, the editor of the series of works entitled *L'Évolution de l'Humanité.*[1] Sociology, in his view, deals only with the social element in history. The *synthèse historique* which he conceives to be the ultimate aim of a scientific history would be more inclusive. According to his theory three sorts of factors can be traced in the historical process which he designates contingence, necessity, and inner or immanent logic. The contingent includes sheer successions, chance events, the rôle of the individual *qua* individual, temporary collective moods, ethnic and geographical conditions. The necessary factors include what are ordinarily called institutions, necessary in the sense that the same fundamental institutions are found everywhere. The logical factor is apparently an expression of the fundamental tendency in all life to maintain itself and to develop. 'Et le principe d'où procédé toute logique, le moteur véritable de l'histoire,—comme de la vie—on ne saurait le trouver, semble-t-il, que dans la tendance a être, a maintenir et à amplifier. La vie n'est pas quelque chose de passif et, pour ainsi dire, de vide ; elle est tendance at elle est mémoire. Quand elle réussit, elle rétient les moyens de sa réussite. La logique, dans le sens étroit du mot, c'est le bon usage de l'esprit ; au sens large, c'est l'activité conforme aux tendances fondamentales de l'être, qui use des moyens appropriés.

[1] *La synthèse en histoire* ; 'Introduction générale' in *La Terre avant l'histoire,* by E. Perrier (first volume of the *L'Évolution de l'Humanité.*

Emanée donc du trefonds de la vie, l'activité logique aboutit a l'entr' aide aussi bien qu'à la lutte, s'épanouit dans l'instinct social plus que dans l'égoïsme,—crée, en définitive, la société elle-même.' [1] Historical synthesis must deal with all these elements. It should cover the whole range of culture, ' les modalités et le progrès de la vie sous la forme humaine, dans les sociétés '. Sociology, on the other hand, is partial and must restrict itself to the social elements in culture. It would seem that, according to him, this term covers the juridico-political and the economic functions of society, but not the strictly intellectual, aesthetic or religious activities of men. Mental development is ' human ', but not strictly social. Religion, again, though strongly socialized is yet *d'essence humaine,* and it is through the reaction of individuals against institutionalized religion that there arise art, philosophy, and science. Historical synthesis, in opposition to sociology, must take account of the rôle of creative and inventive individuals, and above all must seek to bring together the contingent or merely given, the elements involved in society as such—that is to say, institutions—and the inner drive expressed in wants, needs, and reflective volition, which constitutes the logic of historical evolution.

M. Berr's philosophy of history seems to have been worked out in order to provide a plan for the very important series of historical works to which I have referred. It is difficult to say to what extent, if at all, it has affected its contributors. Here we are only concerned with the problem of the relation between sociology and history. In this connexion M. Berr's arguments seem to me open to the objection that when he speaks of sociology he has really in mind only the teaching of Durkheim and his school. M. Berr is no doubt right in stressing the importance of individual

[1] *La synthèse en histoire* ; p. vi seq.

volition and thought. Society, as he says, does not think. It may be important to insist on this as against theories of a group mind or collective representations, though it is doubtful whether even Durkheim thought of these collective representations as inhering anywhere save in individual minds. But once the theory of a collective mind is disposed of, the validity of M. Berr's distinction between the social and the human disappears. It must be urged that intellectual, religious and artistic development are just as much social products as are juridico-economic institutions. Like the latter, they depend on interactions and interrelations between minds in society and on the cumulative processes of tradition. In both the precise contribution of individual initiative is difficult to determine, and remains in any case a problem to be investigated by the sociologist rather than a dogma with which we can safely start on our inquiries. In short, M. Berr seems to me to be taking too narrow a view of sociology; and, what is perhaps more important, he starts with a most ambitious theory of social causation which, to my mind, should be the crowning achievement and not the starting-point of historical and sociological investigation.

Less *a priori* and more in harmony with the actual procedure of historians and sociologists appear to me to be the views of some other very distinguished French historians who have discussed this question. According to Prof. Pirenne [1] the relation between sociology and history is akin to that, say, between economic history and economic theory, or between the history of law and jurisprudence. Prof. Sée [2] thinks sociology deals with social facts *in abstracto*, that is, without reference to any particular space or time. It seeks to ascertain

[1] *La méthode comparative en histoire. Congrès des sciences historiques de Bruxelles*, p. 923.
[2] *Science et philosophie de l'Histoire*, p. 130.

the general conditions of social life and change; while history is concrete and deals with particular events. This view is also shared by Prof. Mantoux.[1] All insist on the close interconnexion of the two disciplines. Sée and Pirenne both emphasize the importance for history of comparative studies, and they see that, in this respect at any rate, it comes very close to the work of the sociologist, for whom the use of the comparative method is essential. Prof. Mantoux points out that the distinction between the study of institutions, which is supposed to be the proper object of sociology, and the study of *événements*, which belongs to the historian, must not be drawn too closely, since we cannot understand institutions without taking into consideration the *événements* from which they start and which accompany the changes they undergo. It would seem that we are dealing rather with a difference in emphasis or stress than with one of fundamental difference of aim. The sociologist is concerned primarily with the discovery of general laws or tendencies of social life; the historian is concerned primarily with the interpretation of concrete or individual occurrences. The business of history, says Prof. Monod [2] is not to be satisfied with the discovery of general conditions, but to show them in operation in specific historical situations. Particularization and generalization cannot, however, be fruitfully dissevered.

With the view here indicated I strongly sympathize. I turn now to a school of thought who wish to emphasize the contrast or antithesis between the individual and universal, and who regard history as concerned with unique, unrepeatable, individual wholes which cannot be studied by the methods of abstraction, comparison, or generalization employed in the social sciences. In

[1] *Histoire et Sociologie. Rev. de synthèse historique*, 1903, t. VII.

[2] G. Monod, 'Histoire', in *De la méthode dans les sciences* (Prémiére Série), 1920.

Germany this tendency goes back to Windelband and his successor Rickert, with whom I cannot here deal. I shall confine myself to one form of this attitude expounded with great force and learning by Troeltsch.[1]

Troeltsch does not in any way wish to minimize the importance of sociology. His conception of it does not differ materially from that expounded at the beginning of this paper. Sociology, he thinks, may be said to consist of the following sub-divisions. In the first place, and in its most general and formal aspect, it deals with the nature and laws of social relationships, as such, irrespective of content. In the second place, these social relationships are embodied in specific manner in each of the great spheres of culture—for example, religion, art, the State. There is accordingly a sociological treatment of each such sphere. Thirdly, we may deal with societies as concrete entities, after the manner of Comte, Spencer, Schäffle. Fourthly, comparative studies of the life of societies and the phases or stages of their development may be made, as, for example, in the work of Schmoller, Breysig, Sombart. Fifthly, there are the problems of *Kultursoziologie*, by which, I take it, he understands an inquiry into the relation between the higher cultural elements and the more massive substructure consisting of the economic and political factors or elements. To this subdivision belongs the work of Max Weber on the sociology of religion, and Troeltsch's own studies in the *Soziallehren*. In all these subdivisions conceptual schemata are arrived at as the result of inductive and comparative studies. From the point of view of the historian they are *Hilfswissenschaften*, which may suggest questions and interpretations to him but cannot do his proper work.

History in Troeltsch's view is the concrete and intuitive representation of individual wholes. These are

[1] E. Troeltsch, *Der Historismus und seine Probleme*.

not capable of interpretation in terms of separable elements in interaction. The individual is 'etwas in lezter Linie lediglich Gesetztes und Tatsächliches, das unauflösliche Geheimnis des Lebens'. The individual is unique, original, and unrepeatable, a sort of emergent not deducible from the nature of its elements in composition. The term is used not in contrast with groups or complexes but with the abstractness of general laws. It can be applied not only to persons but also to collective entities, such as classes, peoples, epochs, events like the Renaissance—anything that can be grasped as a whole by the historian. Each such whole—for example the Israelite people, the Hellenic culture—is a new formation whose nature cannot be explained by reference to psychology, the influence of the environment or heredity and the like, but can only be intuitively *nachgefühlt*. Each such whole, again, has its own *Wesen* or *Sinn, Wert oder Sinneinheit*, which the historian must intuit. To understand a period is to look at it from the point of view of its own ideals and standards. Troeltsch upholds the doctrine of historical relativism. Each period has its own system of values. The business of the historian is to feel himself into his period by a sort of immanent criticism and penetration. His procedure in dealing with a given period or with evolution in history is different from that employed in the natural sciences. It is an effort to obtain an intuitive grasp or apprehension of countless particular processes fused and synthesized into a unique and unanalysable whole. What is to be regarded as such a whole can only be determined by the selective intuition of the historian, and here again he needs a power of sympathetic penetration differing in kind from the power of analysis and construction requisite in the domain of the natural sciences.

It is difficult in a short survey to do justice to Troeltsch's arguments. There can be no doubt that he is right in insisting that history must of necessity start with concrete entities and not with supposed primary atomic elements. There can also be no doubt of the value of the notion of individual wholes, which, to my mind, as actually used by historians are extremely complex concepts summing up the historian's vision of the concrete life of a period or of a group of events. But it may be doubted whether the cognitive processes by which such concepts are constructed really differ in kind from those which are involved in the work of the natural sciences. There is in any event no magical potency in such concepts as the Renaissance, and their explanatory value depends upon the extent to which they embody detailed and painstaking analysis of the forces involved and the possibility of their being ultimately related to the fundamental laws of life and mind. When historians such as Sée, Pirenne, and Tawney [1] examine the value of such concepts as, for example, 'modern capitalism' as used, let us say, by Sombart, or wish to test the accuracy of Troeltsch's or Max Weber's views about the relation between Puritanism and the capitalist mentality, they do not appeal to mysterious intuitions but to evidence derived from a comparative study of the growth of capitalism in the different European countries. They seek to ascertain the composition of the social classes that contributed most to it, or, again, they appeal to supposed psychological laws of the way in which urban life affects the mentality of its inhabitants. In the absence of such detailed analytic studies, the concept of individual wholes, which Troeltsch takes to be the essential instrument of historical explanation, may lead to interesting subjective impressions, but hardly to

[1] cf. Sée, op. cit., Pt. II, Ch. III, Pirenne, 'Les périodes de L'histoire sociale du capitalisme' (*Bull. de l'Academie de Belgique*, 1914), and *Histoire de Belgique*, tt. I and II, Tawney, Foreword to Max Weber's *The Protestant Ethic and the Spirit of Capitalism.*

3

a rational understanding of the phenomena of history. In Troeltsch's own case it has led to one particular conclusion of great significance, to which I should like to draw special attention. It has led him, namely, to deny the historical validity of the concept of humanity or of human evolution. Nothing, in his view, can be treated as a proper subject of history which cannot be grasped as a cultural unity; nothing can properly be said to evolve which does not reveal an underlying unity of culture or spiritual identity throughout the changes which it undergoes. Humanity has no such unity, and we cannot legitimately deal with it as a whole. The historian can only deal with definite *Kultur-kreise*, each of which, in his opinion, has its own *Sinn und Wesen*, unique and not comparable with the *Sinn* and *Wesen* of other culture complexes. I have on another occasion dealt with the problem of evolution in sociology, and have shown that the use of the concept of evolution as applied to humanity can be made perfectly intelligible without appeal to mysterious underlying unities.[1] Here I would only urge that Troeltsch vastly exaggerates the uniqueness and independence of these *Kultur-kreise*, and that the methods whereby each can be studied are essentially alike and appear to reveal agencies in operation in their nature akin throughout the whole of humanity. The notion of the 'individual' as used by Troeltsch is, in any event, far too vague to bear the weight of a conclusion of such vast moment in the discussion of historical evolution. If the concept of humanity does not constitute a unitary notion, neither, I will venture to say, does the concept, say, of the European-American *Kultur-Kreis*, and for the understanding of either, intuition is not enough.

Out of the brief review I have given two problems suggest themselves which require further discussion.

[1] See Chapter IV.

There is, first, the question of the relation between our knowledge of particulars, or rather individuals, and our knowledge of general laws. There is, second, the problem of standards of valuation in historical and sociological interpretation.

It seems widely held that the proper business of history is to describe individual occurrences, or rather complexes of occurrences, while the duty of the social theorist is to discover, if he can, general laws or tendencies, or in any case to construct interpretative conceptual schemata. But there appear to be differences of opinion as to whether we are dealing here with a convenient division of labour or whether there is implied a radical difference of aim and method. A crucial test in this connexion is, I think, found in the attitude adopted to the use of the comparative method. Prof. Sée and Prof. Pirenne certainly advocate its use in history, and have themselves employed it with effect, though they point out that its extensive use belongs rather to sociology than history. According to them, therefore, no hard and fast line can here be drawn. The sociologist is primarily interested in the discovery of general laws; the historian in the interpretation and description of concrete situations and actual sequences. On the other hand, Prof. Berr seeks to make history the more inclusive of two disciplines. But his view, as we have seen, rests upon a doubtful distinction between the generically human and the distinctively social. Troeltsch and many other German writers interpret the distinction between sociology and history as resting upon and as implying a radical difference in the type of knowledge involved in the two cases, the one being an intuitive apprehension of unique totalities, the other utilizing methods of analysis and synthesis akin to those which are familiar in the natural sciences. Is there, then, any real difference between our knowledge of an individual and our knowledge through general laws? Let us consider a simple example. If I say I know a person X I mean, so it seems to me, that he has been presented to me frequently in direct sense-perception, and that from my experience of him I have gathered a cumulative impression which gives me insight into his character. It is extremely likely that if I were to write an account of him I should not be helped much by what I have read in the text-books of psychology. I may, nevertheless, claim to have psychological insight into his make-up, though the word 'psychological' would be here used in a sense which would not satisfy the scientific psychologist. Nevertheless, the business of the psychologist is, it seems to me, ultimately to enable us to understand concrete individuals, X and others, and the failure to achieve this purpose is evidence of the immaturity and imperfection of psychological science. If psychology were more advanced it would help me in knowing X, and I should then have a knowledge of him on a higher level than I have at present when I have to rely on intuitive impressions unchecked by any rigid method. I cannot accept the view, so often put forward now by methodologists, that the ultimate object of science is not the knowledge of the concrete individual but the framing of general laws. Generality and individuality are not in fact mutually exclusive. In using general terms or general laws to describe an individual I bring out the points in which he resembles other individuals, but a thing does not lose individuality by possessing characteristics in common with others or entering into relations with them. There may indeed be something peculiar to each individual. In any event, individuals differ from one another in countless ways. But that what remains after we have exhausted our analysis of an individual in general terms is a residuum immune from the methods of reason and requiring a mystical intuition, is an assumption for which no satisfactory evidence has been offered. Ultimately, it seems to me, it is in and through particulars that we discern the universal, and in this sense there is an empirical element in all science, however abstract. Sciences of course vary considerably in the degree of their generality and abstractness. It is even possible, and indeed desirable in some cases, to work out deductive schemes bringing out the implications of certain assumptions without reference for the time being to the truth of these assumptions. This is the case in some branches of mathematics, and, according to some authorities, even in physics. In the social sciences too such procedure is important. It is done, for example, in pure economic theory, though here the assumptions, as I understand, are of the nature of psychological generalizations regarding human motives. Conceivably economic theories might be worked out, starting from different assumptions, and their consequences deduced simply as a study in possibilities. In linguistics students distinguish between general linguistics, which investigates the general possibilities of speech, and special or historical linguistics, which is concerned with the specific ways in which these possibilities are actualized under varying historical conditions. I take it that the assumptions made in general linguistics are based on generalizations derived from anatomy, physiology, and psychology. On the other hand, special linguistics is in part a sociological study, since there appears to be a close relation between the development of language and the forms of social structure, as has been pointed out especially by Meillet.[1]

In sociology, again, we have seen the attempt has been made to build up a pure science of social forms, though the method has not so far proved very fruitful.

[1] A. Meillet, *Linguistique historique et linguistique générale*, pp. 44 seq.

It is arguable that purely deductive studies in the social sciences are richer in possibilities than we are accustomed to think, especially if use can be made of the more accurate methods of analysis provided by modern logic.

If the social sciences could be content with such purely deductive studies, their relation to history would of course be very remote. But without disputing the value of such theoretical studies in any way, I should like to urge that in sociology in particular it is vitally important not to separate too sharply the study of forms from the concrete study of contents. The assumptions that are used in the social sciences are rarely of the nature of axioms, but are really in most cases unconscious generalizations capable of, and requiring, verification. But this we are apt to forget. The result is that we tend to accept the conclusions based on them as true, whereas in fact they are merely consistent deductions validly drawn perhaps but not necessarily applicable to real fact. It is thus of the greatest importance to revise our assumptions in the light of verifiable fact. Moreover, in sociology the material we have to deal with is in its very nature historical, that is, dependent on tradition and the cumulative action of past events. Further, if there is any one well substantiated generalization in the study of culture, it is that cultural development is stimulated by contact, and depends on the opportunities available for borrowing and diffusion. To trace diffusion is the work of the historian. This was very clearly brought out by Maitland, who showed its importance to anthropology, and is a matter upon which great emphasis is laid by the so-called historical school of anthropology. It is sometimes thought that history and sociology are in the last resort nothing but applied psychology. If there is any truth in this, we should have to regard psychology not as a science which deals with a supposedly constant human nature, but with a human nature that undergoes change in the course of human development. It will then be seen that the causes which affect the varying expression of human nature are to be found in conditions which are not themselves of a psychological character and cannot be studied by the methods of the psychologist. It is clear, for instance, that however intimate our knowledge may be of the psychology of sex and of the parental-filial relation, it will not of itself suffice to explain the varied forms of family structure or the laws and customs regulating the relations between the sexes. The variations in the rules forbidding marriage between near kin cannot be explained by reference to a uniform human nature. They depend upon conditions which must be traced historically in each case. Neglect of this consideration will undoubtedly lead us often to assume that a particular attitude is based upon an inborn or instinctive tendency in human nature which in fact is the product of development and is susceptible of modification in a new environment. In short, the functional analysis of human institutions, their physiology and psychology, so to speak, must be in its nature historical and evolutionary. Purely deductive studies of the possibilities of human nature may have their value, but at some point they must be brought to the test of inductive and comparative study and related to the actual course of social evolution.

If social theory cannot fruitfully be divorced from social history, the converse proposition is equally true. In actual practice, historians do not confine themselves to narration or detailed description, but inquire into causes and not infrequently indulge in generalizations of vast extent and import. The importance of theory is often consciously recognized and even stressed by historians. In a recent article Sombart has made a powerful plea for the need of co-operation between economic theory and economic history. He claims that his own work, which seeks to ascertain the common elements in the various forms of European capitalism, is both history and theory. Max Weber's use of the notion of ' types ' may be similarly so regarded. Vinogradoff's work in historical jurisprudence is partly historical, partly sociological. He deals not only with the origins of legal forms, but also with the value-judgments which they embody and the compromises and adjustments which they express.[1] I may also refer to Prof. Sée's work on agrarian conditions in Europe in the eighteenth and nineteenth centuries, which is essentially comparative and sociological, and much other recent work on European capitalism. Even von Below, who attacks the use of the comparative method in history very fiercely,[2] in the end admits its usefulness, at any rate, as likely to stimulate inquiry and suggest new hypotheses. The very cautious Langlois and Seignobos concede that the method is useful negatively in the disproof, for example, of alleged connexions, such as between Christianity and the favourable position of women.[3] But the use of the comparative method implies I think, a theory of social causation, at least in the sense that it postulates the possibility of disentangling identical or similar relevant conditions from among complex situations which as wholes differ vastly from each other. History and sociology are thus intrinsically related to each other.

Before further defining their relationship, I will say a few words with regard to the second problem to which reference was made above, namely, that of the relation between history and standards of value. Two things

[1] Paul Vinogradoff, *Custom and Right*; *Historical Jurisprudence*.

[2] Below, op. cit., p. 21.

[3] Langlois and Seignobos, *Introduction to the Study of History*, p. 291.

appear to me pretty clear. In the first place, the historian and the sociologist cannot exclude from their domain all reference to values. There is such a thing as the historical and comparative study, for example, of moral and religious ideas, and the conditions of their evolution can be studied by the same methods as those which are employed in the investigation of social institutions generally. Moreover, in so far as beliefs in values are possibly agents which influence human behaviour, their causal efficacy in relation to other factors involved in the historical process forms a legitimate and necessary part of historical synthesis and sociological generalization. In the second place, it is frequently pointed out that the historian can not, and perhaps ought not to, avoid judgments of valuation either in the selection of his data or in estimating the relative importance of the varying processes which he investigates. In this connexion it should be realized that the historian's value-judgments are themselves historically conditioned and are subject to what has been called 'historical relativity'.[1] Yet the history and sociology of values cannot take the place of ethics, aesthetics, or social philosophy. These disciplines must of course start with the actual judgments that men make of the beautiful, the good, and the true. But their methods for testing the validity of these judgments are not, as such, psychological or historical, but follow a procedure directed at the discovery of the fundamental principles which would make our actual judgments coherent and consistent. Ethics cannot be reduced to the comparative study of moral ideas any more than logic can be reduced to psychology and sociology. Social philosophy has thus a field of its own which cannot be identified either with history or sociology.

[1] Bury, *Selected Essays*. 'Ancient Greek Historians'; 'Idea of Progress.'

To sum up. The view that sociology and history differ in the kind of knowledge they seek to attain does not appear to be well substantiated. The knowledge of the universal and the knowledge of the particular are inseparably intertwined. The claim that history deals only with individual and unrepeatable occurrences is not really in harmony with the actual procedure of historians. In economic and social history especially events are studied which recur quite frequently, and which exhibit sufficient similarity of structure to render possible generalized treatment. Comparative and typological studies are indeed becoming very frequent in economic history. The notion of the individual is in any event very vaguely used in this connexion. In a sense everything that happens is singular or unique, but this does not prevent us from studying individuals in the points in which they exhibit resemblance. The lover, it has been well said,[1] believes that his experience is unique and unlike the experience of any one else. But is his *unio mystica* really beyond the reach of science? On the other hand, the sociologist cannot admit that he must confine himself to generalities or abandon the study of societies in the concrete. The difference between the sociologist and the historian is thus one merely of emphasis. The primary interest of the one is the discovery of general laws, of the other the reconstruction of the way in which events have actually occurred. In respect of the problem of valuation, sociology and history appear to me to be in the same position *vis-à-vis* social philosophy. They are not concerned with the truth or validity of value-judgments. They are of service to the social philosopher in supplying him with data and in encouraging an active and healthy scepticism, but they cannot do his work for him.

[1] Franz Eulenberg, 'Sind historische Gesetze möglich', in *Eauptprobleme der Soziologie*. Erinnerungsgabe, für Max Weber, p. 31.

I should like in conclusion to make a practical suggestion. Sociology has been, as it seems to me, somewhat too much preoccupied with the study of primitive peoples, and has not made adequate use of the vast stores of historical knowledge. There is great need at present for an extension of the field of the comparative study of institutions. It is of especial importance that use should be made of the scientific technique elaborated by modern historians, so that perchance the somewhat too ready generalizations of some of the earlier sociologists may be avoided. To this end I should like to suggest that historians and sociologists co-operate in the preparation of a series which might perhaps be called *Notes and Queries in the Comparative Study of Institutions*. This should provide a list of sources, a classification of social institutions, and a discussion of the main problems that arise in connexion with them, so far as they lend themselves to comparative study. Perhaps this Congress, which has given us the opportunity for ventilating the whole question of the relation between sociology and history, will increase our indebtedness to it by initiating or encouraging such an enterprise.

III

SOCIAL PURPOSE

THE social sciences all more or less explicitly use the notion of purpose. Some, as, for example, Economics and Law, are based on certain assumptions as to the nature of human motives and are directly concerned with consciously purposive behaviour. Others, for example, Anthropology and Ethnology, frequently employ teleological modes of explanation in a manner more familiar in the biological sciences. Thus customs and institutions generally are discussed from the point of view of their survival value (or other social function) to the groups or peoples among whom they spring up. Groups are said to persist as wholes, to exhibit plasticity and adaptability and other features of the organic world. In the wider sciences of Sociology and Politics we speak of a social purpose and a social good, and the analogy between social wholes and individual persons or organisms is frequently debated. I propose here to inquire how far and in what sense social wholes are purposive, and into the relation between the purposive and the organic, as these terms are used when they are applied to societies.

(*a*) The idea of purpose, in ordinary usage, appears to rest on our experience of the higher forms of voluntary activity. It implies (i) an idea or conception of the present state of affairs and in contrast therewith an idea or representation of a state of affairs as yet non-existent, (ii) the formation of a plan and the selection of the means or instruments necessary to bring about the desired change, (iii) conative-affective elements issuing finally in the act of will proper whereby the plan is carried into execution. Purposive activity is accordingly most naturally interpreted as consisting in the realization of a preconceived plan. Very little reflection, however, is needed to show that this is an inadequate account of even the higher forms of purposive activity, where the notion of a plan is most prominent.

(i) This view exaggerates the extent to which conscious factors are operative in voluntary activity. A voluntary act seems to be the expression of the deep-seated and massive impulses of our nature, and these exert an influence which is often not at all, or only dimly, realized by the agent. Herein perhaps is the reason why our actions exhibit an immanent purposiveness which often goes beyond conscious choice and deliberate control. (ii) We speak of artistic and intellectual work as purposive, but in them the purpose grows, changes, and develops with the execution of the work. Poetic or musical inspiration can hardly be described as a progressive and orderly adaptation of means to ends. Process and result cannot here be separated. The whole seems to be the expression of a more or less unconscious urge. The whole determines the parts, but that whole is not consciously realized at the outset. This is true even of more definitely intellectual work. (iii) Even in practical activity, the end we set ourselves changes as we proceed to realize it. New circumstances arise, the agent himself alters in nature as he proceeds, and thus results are often achieved which were never foreseen or intended. It follows from this 'heterogony of ends', as Wundt has called it, that in a sense the end is determined by the means, just as the means are determined by the end. The true nature of the process is not realized until the end is achieved, and the end is only seen in the process as actually realized. (iv) The category of purpose is constantly used in biology in reference to the lower organisms, but I suppose no one would maintain that these, or for that matter man himself, have a preconceived plan of their own existence and of the functions of their parts. The interpretation of purpose as consisting in the realization of an antecedent plan is natural enough when applied to cases of the execution of an order or command or to machines which realize purposes intended by their maker, but it is clearly inadequate as a complete account.

(*b*) It is thus natural that purposiveness should come to be brought under or identified with the wider notion of teleology. Now, teleology is sometimes regarded as a category co-ordinate with other forms of causality, whilst at other times it seems to be contrasted with causality. This appears to be due to an ambiguous use of the latter term, which may be taken to mean determination by conditions which can be stated in mechanical terms, and which properly applies to events or processes occasioned by a redistribution of energy within a physical system, or it may be used more generally to refer to the determination of an event or process by any set of conditions, not necessarily mechanical. For example, vital or mental elements may be held not to be completely explicable in terms of mechanics, yet they may be constituents of a set of conditions which cause or determine an event. If cause is used in the wider sense just referred to, teleology may be regarded as a species of causality.

(i) *Determination by the Future.*—Teleology is often said to operate *a fronte*, while other forms of causality operate *a tergo*. But this seems to ignore the fact that in a teleological whole, the end is in a sense just as determined by the means as the means by the end. Furthermore, it involves a denial of the reality of the temporal process. If time is real, all causality must be *a tergo*.[1]

[1] cf. Prof. Alexander, *Space, Time and Deity*, Vol. I, p. 287.

But in truth the phenomena of voluntary behaviour, which at first sight suggest that in some sense an event in the future influences the present act, need no interpretation incompatible with the view that in causal actions it is the present conditions which are continuous with and determine the future. When I run to catch a train what moves me is a present act of thought which has for its content an event in the future. The determinant is the present act of thought or rather the impulse connected with or accompanying it. Indeed, the event contemplated, my catching the train, may not actually happen, for I may miss it.

(ii) We are thus led to substitute for the phrase, determination by the future, determination by a *tendency* to produce a result. An action is held to be teleological when it is set in motion by its own tendency to produce a result. The term tendency is used also in regard to physical agents when we wish to indicate that certain conditions have a character such that in the absence of counteracting conditions they give rise to an effect. But this does not seem to be the sense in which the term is used when applied to teleological actions. It implies nisus or effort or impulse and a certain amount of prospective reference. To this I shall return. Meanwhile we must note another feature of purposive action, namely, that it is in some sense a whole or organization. The series of events which enter into a purposive act are held together by the governing impulse to produce a result, and they are varied, maintained, or dropped, according as they do or do not tend to that result.

(iii) *Determination by the Whole.*—Thus teleological wholes are said to have a more intimate unity than that which belongs to mechanical wholes. In a mechanical whole the parts form a system or differentiated unity, but they are so related that each acts uniformly without relation to the rest, in response to the force immediately operating on it and independently of the results of its action. The parts are, so to speak, complete in themselves, independent and indifferent. In organic activity and in purposive behaviour the parts are determined by, and vary with, the requirements of the whole.[1] But this distinction does not seem to me very clear. For one thing, some machines may be so delicately constructed and their parts so interdependent that the parts can only function together and in such a manner that a breakdown anywhere stops the whole. A machine, however, is not a good case, for of course it *is* a teleological whole. When we take other mechanical systems it is by no means obvious that the parts are indifferent. Moreover, does not the argument imply rather too sharp a severance of cause from effect ? Any part of a machine will work, it is said, so long as there is a force operating upon it, whatever source it may come from. Now, no doubt the wheel of a bicycle will move whether the chain be pulled by hand or by the other wheel, but as total physical events the movement will be different in the one case from the other. Again, organic and even purposive activity may be regarded as determined by causes operating immediately ; for varied conduct is determined by variation in stimuli and in conative impulses. Further, mental and purposive action may be indifferent in the sense of not being affected by its effects on elements outside the system within which it operates. It seems to me, therefore, that if the organic differs from the mechanical, the difference must lie in the kind of factors through which the 'requirement of the whole' is served. Both are wholes, and in both the nature of the system as a whole must be considered in accounting for changes within it, but in the former, conational factors enter in such a way that the requirement of the whole expresses itself as

[1] cf. Prof. Hobhouse, *Proc. Arist. Soc.*, XVIII, p. 473.

a felt uneasiness setting up varied activities which persist until it is removed. A purposive whole is one in which the activities of the parts are determined by a felt tendency to produce results affecting the whole. This tendency may vary from what amounts to no more than a vague feeling of disturbance of equilibrium to a definitely conceived and articulate system of purposes. A complete account of purposive activity would distinguish different levels of conation and different kinds of conational wholes. We may define a conational whole as one of which the parts strive after mutual adjustment, unity and cohesion. The degree of unity or integration actually attained and the explicitness with which the end is realized by the parts vary enormously from case to case. Whether organisms are conative wholes is much disputed. According to the mechanists the mutual adjustment of parts exhibited by organisms may be explained in terms which are used in dealing with chemical or physical equilibria ; while the vitalists hold that the phenomena of organic life cannot be explained without recourse to some directive agency. Negatively the position of the latter seem to be strong ; they seem to have shown conclusively that mechanistic explanation in the narrowest sense (which regards all phenomena as nothing but determinate and computable configurations and motions) is not adequate to the facts of life and mind. On the other hand, to account for vital integration by recourse to the agency of a vital force acting upon the bodily processes, and similarly to account for the unity of conscious experience by calling in the aid of a substantial soul, is simply to 'restate the characteristic nature of the facts and hypostatize it as a causal *prius* of its own existence'.[1] It seems better to regard the integration exhibited in life and mind as due not to a separate

[1] Prof. Pringle Pattison, *The Idea of Immortality*, p. 113.

entity acting upon and interfering with or modifying the bodily processes, but rather as the result of the interaction of elements which make up the psychophysical whole. In other words, according to this view we regard living beings as exhibiting a new form of correlation of the parts of a system, a new form of integration qualitatively different from the kind of unification that can be seen in systems that are merely mechanical. Perhaps the cells of metazoa are themselves conative,[1] and if so organisms are conative wholes in the sense above referred to, and their unity is the result of the striving of its parts after mutual adjustment. The unity achieved is of course not complete even in highly developed organisms. 'We know,' says Dr. Rivers, 'that the living body is the seat of conflicts between forces of many different kinds, that various secretions of the body have actions antagonistic to one another, and that the apparent harmony of the body is due to a highly delicate process of adjustment whereby a balance is held between these conflicting forces.'[2] Physiologically a motor act or idea seems to be the expression of some sort of neural equilibrium resulting from the action and interaction of the parts of the cortex and the reverberation of nervous activity from one association centre to another.[3] We have here a new integration whose precise nature is not understood. A higher level of integration is seen in the holding together of the various processes of consciousness in a single or individual stream. In this case also the unity achieved varies considerably and may well be of the nature of a balance of elements striving after mutual adjustment.

When we pass from the organism to organic activity or behaviour we meet with phenomena which imply

[1] cf. Prof. Hobhouse, ibid., p. 474.
[2] *Psychology and Politics*, p. 57.
[3] cf. Herrick, *Introduction to Neurology*, p. 329.

active striving, tentative effort, selective preference, prospective reference, and progressive organization, which are indicative of the growth of mind and of its nisus towards co-ordination and unity. A comparative study of behaviour enables us to mark out conational unities of different degrees of coherence, articulateness, comprehensiveness, and plasticity. All are characterized by the fact that they are systems of elements or processes, which have a temporal individuality and which exhibit such varied effort and adjustment of part to part as serves to maintain and prolong that individuality. The adjustment may be no more than a balance of conflicting elements, just sufficient somehow to preserve the system as a whole, and may even involve a great deal of suppression, or it may be delicately harmonized, satisfying the conation of each element and at the same time maintaining the whole. In such cases we have a system in which the parts are truly means and ends to one another. Possibly only approximations to this ideal type exist. The harmonious unity of the whole is the final end of the system, but it is only in the higher phases of correlation or integration that the end enters into clear consciousness. Teleological wholes, then, are conational; they consist of parts which severally and with varying degrees of awareness strive after mutual adjustment. Purposive wholes in the narrower sense are a species of this wider genus.

(iv) Teleology is sometimes explained by reference to the idea of value. It is said that a nexus of cause and effect can be looked upon as also a nexus of means to end, whenever the effect has *value*. This is an interesting theory, but I doubt whether as a causal agent, at least from the point of view of the organism concerned, value can be satisfactorily explained apart from some reference to satisfied conation, and we are thus brought back to the view suggested above.

(c) We may now inquire whether and in what sense the category of purpose applies to social wholes. There are many different kinds of social wholes, varying enormously in permanence, coherence, plasticity, differentiation, and unity. In recent discussions it has become customary to distinguish between society or community and association. The former refers to a group of social beings living a common life, and includes all the relations organized and unorganized that make up that common life. The latter term is used to refer to groupings which exist for specific purposes or functions and are therefore partial forms of community. They vary in comprehensiveness, scale, and duration with the character of the purposes which they subserve. I propose to confine attention here to community as an integral whole and leave aside the question of the nature of the partial associations or other groupings within it.

(i) *Continuity*.—Communities maintain themselves as continuous wholes, resist injuries, and exhibit plasticity of adjustment in the face of a varying environment.[1] This can be seen in various ways. Firstly, there is spatial continuity due to a life in a given area marked off from other areas. This need not be laboured. The importance of a definite home country to the unity of a people is obvious. Definite attachment to a given locality is important even for minor associations. For example, the family owed a great deal of its stability at some periods of its history to the fact it was attached to a house or piece of land that was not often alienated, and its disintegration is at least partly due to the greater mobility of its members occasioned by changes in the industrial system and the consequent breaking of local ties. Secondly, there is the temporal and physiological continuity of generations. In any community there is never any moment of which we can say

[1] cf. Simmel, *Soziologie*.

that in it an entirely new generation begins. The change is gradual and continuous, and the number of new elements arriving at any one moment is small in proportion to the mass that remains. Thirdly, not only does one generation pass into another, but it transmits its qualities, physical and mental, through the influence of heredity. Thus a race or nation comes to have a set of characteristics exhibited more or less continuously in successive generations. The unity and continuity thus attained must not, however, be exaggerated. Many attempts have been made to explain social history in terms of a special character or temperament or predisposition supposed to be immanent in each race and manifesting itself in their institutions. These attempts have taken many forms, and they have a way of reappearing in different guise as new classifications of races come and go. Detailed study invariably seems to show their inadequacy. They break down completely, for example, when applied to legal history,[1] and they come no less to grief when used to explain the national peculiarities of literature and art or religion, or such social phenomena as the frequency of divorce and suicide. They at once exaggerate and over-simplify the unity and continuity of social life, and ignore the fact that national or social unity is integrative and creative, a resultant of the action and interaction of many and varied forces in contact with a varying environment. The real agents of social change are not racial or ethnic, but social, though the former may act as contributory causes in accelerating social or traditional changes. With these qualifications, physiological heredity is an important factor in the conditions upon which depends the continuity of the life of a people. A fourth and more important factor is social as distinguished from

[1] cf. Roscoe Pound, *Interpretations of Legal History*, Chap. VI.

biological heredity. Communities create for themselves a tradition, a system of beliefs, institutions, and organizations which have a permanence and an efficacy greater than that which belongs to any individual. In this connexion too there is a tendency to exaggerate the degree of unity attained. It is only too easy to assume that an institution which exists to-day is the same as that which was called by the same name hundreds of years ago, or that in all institutions there is a definite principle expressing constant and permanent needs of human nature. The truth is that institutions change in character and function and that their identity in the flux of time is largely illusory—the illusion being due to the fact that we often cannot point to any definite act replacing by one stroke the old by the new. This is particularly clear in the case of legal institutions, which change gradually by a 'succession of crumblings,[1] repairings, partial replacings, remodellings, and additions'—an adaptive process of trial and error. It should also be noted, as Lotze has pointed out,[2] that, though the effect of tradition is continuous and cumulative, there is a great deal that cannot be transmitted. 'The elevating freshness and joyousness, full of prophetic insight, that distinguish an age of invention and discovery, are not transmitted to the ages that are its heirs. Scientific truths, hardly-won principles of social morality, revelations of religious enthusiasm and artistic intuition, are all subject to this devitalization; the greater the amount of this wealth which is transmitted to later generations, the less is it a living possession, even when distinctly recognized and retained, which it not always is."

(ii) *Interdependence of Parts.*—Communities vary considerably in the closeness of connexion that exists

[1] cf. Roscoe Pound, ibid., p. 39.
[2] *Microcosmos II*, English translation, p. 151.

between their parts. Some are only held together very loosely. Some, aptly described by Durkheim as segmentary, consist of little more than reduplications of similar parts, without any central controlling principle and resembling the lower metameric organisms. Others, more highly organized, consist of parts which are functionally complementary and possess a great deal of central control. The interconnexion is most obvious in the industrial systems of advanced nations. The series of industrial processes of which they consist exhibit an extraordinary number of connecting bonds, both of union and opposition, and though they may appear at first sight to be running each a completely isolated course, they in fact cross, fuse, and separate at various points and in a sense constitute an integral whole. Transport and finance in particular are pervasive and connective and give continuity to the whole movement. A similar interconnexion can be seen in the mutual influence exerted by the various sciences and arts upon one another and upon the general life of a people. This interconnexion is deeply rooted in the relation between the individual and society. Not only are individuals endowed with social impulses which need other members of society for their realization or satisfaction, but the contents of the individual mind are largely social in character in the sense that they come to be known by them as the result of social interaction. Indeed, the consciousness of self develops through intersubjective intercourse. Even conflicts between individuals are to some extent social, arise out of social interaction, and the most difficult to solve are those which are inspired by group feeling or group selfishness. Communities arise and maintain themselves in response to common needs and the pressure of common desires and purposes which cannot be fulfilled except through co-operation. Individuals are essentially and intrinsically related to one another, and the development of individuality and of sociality go on together.

(iii) *Persistence with Varied Effort and Equilibration.*—Communities have remarkable powers of resisting injuries and of adapting themselves to changing circumstances. In the face of danger, for example, old institutions will be utilized to serve new purposes, and a reorganization of social elements may take place to meet emergencies. In normal times also there is a great deal of plasticity in the life of communities, though, of course, not all communities are equally plastic. The process of adjustment moves towards an equilibrium. Thus, for example, in industry there is, as economists tell us, a movement towards equilibrium both in production and consumption. A similar process may be observed in the reaction of a society to a great invention or other sudden change. Diffusion takes place gradually, and society again attains a sort of equilibrium. The most interesting phenomena in this connexion are perhaps the changes that come about in the life of a people as the result of changes in the control of nature and in material culture generally. Changes in the quantity of population seem also to point to a kind of moving equilibrium. According to some authorities [1] there is a tendency for population to reach an optimum density, that is a density which, taking into account, on the one hand, the known arts of production, and, on the other, the habits of a people at any given time, will be the most desirable from the point of view of return per head of the population.

(iv) *Growth and Development.*—The process of equilibration seems closely connected with growth. Communities grow by continuously shifting or moving their equilibrium. Development takes place gradually by a

[1] cf. Carr-Saunders, *The Population Problem*, pp. 200 seq.

process of natural multiplication and outward expansion, by extending the area of organization, and by a rearrangement of elements within the community. In so far as there is genuine growth, there is a liberation of energy hitherto suppressed, and co-operation where hitherto there had been conflict. The most primitive communities of whom we have information live in very small groups and in comparative isolation. Gradually organization expands and covers greater and greater areas. This is at first achieved through military power, and is maintained by authoritarian means. But large-scale organizations which depend entirely on force do not seem to succeed in the long run, unless there also takes place a process of inner unification calling forth the willing response and co-operation of its constituent members. Thus periods during which great States are formed by military conquest are generally succeeded by periods of disintegration and the formation of small States, which only attain ultimate unity after long and painful preparation. Inner integration is just as important as outward expansion. Those communities are more developed which allow a fuller and richer life to their members, which have more voluntary organizations within them, which encourage individuality and initiative. A survey of human history seems to point to a progressive, though not continuous, movement towards the integration and unification of humanity; the formation of wider and yet wider unities—whether we take as our criterion extension of scale of organization or inner unity.

(*d*) Having discussed the most important characteristics of communities, we may now return to the question whether they can be regarded as conative wholes. This is a wider term than organism. We have to recognize many different kinds of conative wholes among organisms themselves. Some are only very low unities—

for example, those constituted by colonies of cells—others consist of reduplications of similar parts. Again, they differ enormously in complexity and differentiation of function and in the degree of central control. Societies can be similarly classified, on the basis of their complexity, differentiation, and the amount of central control. Both societies and organisms vary greatly as regards inner harmony and the presence or absence of conflict and obstruction. On the other hand, while in the higher organisms the parts tend to lose their independence, the contrary is the case in regard to societies. The latter consist of parts which are themselves individual organisms. Accordingly the parts have much greater mobility and are exposed to more varied external influences than are the parts of an individual organism which are physically closely interconnected. The higher societies are therefore more plastic than the higher organisms. Another important difference arises from the fact that a developed community is *communitas communitatum* and includes within itself a multiplicity of associations, groups within groups, in bewildering variety. Individuals may and do belong to a large number of these associations. Moreover, the relations that bind individuals to their associations vary in intensity and importance, according to the purposes which the associations serve. The cells of an organism cannot similarly form part of different systems. Again, the more highly developed a community, the greater the number of its voluntary associations and the greater the freedom possessed by individuals to move from one association to another within or even without the community. (Note, however, that not all associations permit this freedom. For example, one cannot be a citizen of more than one State.) Further, the parts of a community are more readily interchangeable. Functions at one time fulfilled by a particular section of society may at another be fulfilled by quite other bodies. The claim to be 'a harmonious equipotential system' in which '*Jedes kann Jedes*', that Driesch makes for individual organisms at certain stages of their development, has not, I understand, been substantiated,[1] but it could with more plausibility be made for social wholes, owing to the greater plasticity and modifiability of the parts. It should also be remembered that the mutuality and interpenetration of parts is even in the higher communities very imperfect and the diffusion of welfare very unequal. Moral barbarism, mental obtuseness, and physical wretchedness are found side by side with the refinements of life, high intellectual development, and a clear sense of the purposes of human life. There is much conflict due to ignorance and, in part, real incompatibility of needs. There is much obstruction due to indifference. Apart from these differences, there is the important fact that there is no evidence whatever in favour of the existence of a collective consciousness, analogous to the individual consciousness. We have, it seems to me, to recognize integrations of different orders or levels, and the kind of integration exhibited by social wholes is not the same as that which characterizes the holding together of mental processes in one stream of consciousness. Social wholes are, however, organic and conational in the sense that they are wholes which maintain themselves as such by the efforts of their parts towards mutual adjustment. They all reveal a nisus towards wholeness. The historical process embodies the conscious and unconscious efforts of a plurality of individuals to form wider and yet wider wholes. Institutions and tradition generally may be regarded as the result of these efforts. They arise out of the interaction of many minds, in response to the pressure of mutual needs and wants,

[1] cf. Jennings, *Philosophical Review*, 1918, p. 585.

and are trial and error experiments towards mutual adjustment. They are not, as a rule, the result of clearly thought out purposes. The facts of social life and history do not point to the existence of a preconceived plan or unitary purpose, steadily carried out by a unitary mind, but to an advancing organization painfully achieved, through the efforts and struggles of generations of individuals. Nor is the unity attained that of a pre-established harmony independent of the minds of individuals. It is rather a unity of becoming, a process of integration or creative synthesis. The purpose of the whole, if we may speak of one, itself grows and is modified in the course of this process of synthesis; for it consists of an organization of human potentialities and human strivings, and implies continual reciprocal action, surrender and accommodation, the interweaving and modification of individual aims and desires, determined only in part by the conditions of ultimate harmony. Even those who look at history as a process in which an impersonal spirit is realizing itself do not claim that this final aim of history is made a distinct object of desire and interest on the part of individuals. What moves them are their own interests and cravings. 'Nothing,' says Hegel, 'has been accomplished without interest on the part of the actors . . . nothing great in the world has been accomplished without *passion*.'[1] Indeed, unless the strivings of individuals are regarded as real causes, then they become but means and instruments utilized by the 'cunning of Reason' for purposes not theirs and even against their own will; and this is actually maintained by Hegel, at least in one phase of his teaching.[2] If individuals, however, are ends in themselves, then the final end cannot be external to them, but must consist in a mode of life lived by them, not anything preconceived and predetermined,

[1] *Philosophy of History*, p. 24. [2] Ibid., p. 28.

but something that grows and develops as the result of the striving and interaction between individuals 'out of the bliss and despair, the admiration and loathing, the love and the hate, the joyous certainty and the despairing longing, and all the nameless fear and favour in which that life passes which alone is worthy to be called life.[1]'

In any particular case it may be exceedingly difficult to determine the nature of the final causes involved. It is but too easy to assume that the result that actually follows upon a given social process was that intended by the individuals concerned to bring it about. But experience shows that if we try to reason from present functions to past intentions we are almost certainly mistaken. Laws in particular seldom bring about the results which were expected from them when they were being drawn up. Institutions, like individual actions, are characterized by an amazing 'heterogony of ends.' Their functions seem often to change without the intervention of a directing will. 'The human will,' says Tourtoulon,[2] is *a* juridical cause, but it is nothing more than a cause. It urges the law to the right or left, it knows not whither. Must we compare it to Luther's tipsy peasant who cannot stay on his donkey, but falls sometimes to one side, sometimes to the other? This would perhaps be giving it too much honour, for the peasant knows that he has a road and wishes to follow it, although he cannot. The juridical will has no road to follow. It goes, as the poet says, 'où va toute chose, où va la feuille de rose et la feuille de laurier'. In this perhaps there is some exaggeration, though it seems true that if we take long periods of history, social efforts do not exhibit a purposiveness beyond that involved in the stage of trial and error. Another difficulty in the

[1] Lotze, *Microcosmos II*, p. 167.
[2] *Philosophy in the Development of Law.*

study of final causes in the social process arises from the frequent confusion of mediate with ultimate ends, and from the fact that for various psychological reasons means come to be regarded as ends and pursued with an energy and devotion only appropriate to ends. Finally, and especially in the case of the great personages of history, the difficulties in the way of interpreting motives are enhanced by the fact that the ' psychological valets ', as Hegel says, tend to bring down their heroes ' to a level with—or rather a few degrees below the level of—the morality of such exquisite discerners of spirits ', and thus to misunderstand the real nature of the purposes which guided them.

IV

THE CONCEPT OF EVOLUTION IN SOCIOLOGY

THE concept of evolution which, since Tylor and Spencer, has dominated sociological inquiry, has recently been subjected to fierce criticism and there is a growing group of anthropologists and sociologists who reject it as inapplicable to the phenomena of social life. I propose here to examine into the grounds of these attacks and to inquire whether evolutionary notions have really, as is alleged, outlived their ultility in sociology. The opposition comes from different sources and is supported by arguments of very unequal value. In the first part of this paper I will deal with these *seriatim*, and in the second and, I hope, more constructive, part I propose to attempt a reinterpretation of the idea of evolution as used in sociology.

A.—(1) In part, the hostility to evolutionary ideas and methods expresses a not unwarranted discontent with the excessive preoccupation with morphological analysis and classification characteristic of the work of some of the earlier sociologists. A like discontent may be noted in post-Darwinian biology. Here, too, the complaint is frequently heard that research has remained too long dominated by the ideal of tracing phylogeny, has given far too much time to detailed morphology, and has neglected inquiries into process and function.[1] There can be no question that in the study of culture the mistake has sometimes been made of imagining that the full nature of social phenomena

[1] cf. Prof. Tansley, B.A., Report, 1923.

can be stated in terms of their history or origin. It may be added that in sociology, perhaps to a greater extent than in biology, it is important not to separate morphology from physiology. Take, for example, monogamous marriage. It is clearly a different thing when connected with a system of magical taboos, when conceived as an ordinance of the Gospel, or again as an ethical law held necessary in the interests of society. While resembling each other in outward form, the three types of monogamy differ in the sociological forces they rest upon and the functions and purposes which they serve. In short, useful social morphology must take account, not only of external homology, but of inner structure and function. From this point of view, a great deal in the older evolutionary sociology seems rightly open to objection. The point is perhaps most easily illustrated from the treatment of forms of property where the use of such terms as 'communal', 'individual', especially when applied to primitive peoples, frequently leads to the lumping together of institutions of very different nature. Functional analysis is thus obviously important even from the point of view of morphological classification, and the tracing of genetic affinities. It seems to me, however, to be a mistake to erect a sort of antithesis between the functional method and the evolutionary and historical points of view. They are both necessary and are complementary to each other.

(2) In the second place, objection is frequently raised against the purely hypothetical reconstructions of the 'first stages' of institutions, of religious and moral ideas, in which evolutionary sociologists are apt to indulge. The theory of primitive promiscuity is a good example of this kind of speculative reconstruction, inspired by the assumption that in early societies sexual relations are likely to have been 'undifferentiated'.

But I think this objection can be brought forward with much greater reason against what is now sometimes called 'the historical school'. The evolutionary procedure, as I understand it, is not to assume an original type and deduce existing types therefrom. It is to regard every type as an adaptation of social life to meet certain conditions. Its object is to discover the genetic affinities of these types whereby they pass into one another in response to changes of conditions. The important thing here to discover is what is fundamental and what accidental, and, again, what is permanent and what modifiable. If this could be done, we might perhaps have a basis for inferring the types which would be found under conditions more primitive than any of which we have a record. But it is clear that from the evolutionary point of view we should not use these suppositions as starting-points for a theory which is to explain the facts. They are rather conclusions, and are likely to be among the most doubtful conclusions, of a theory already formed. In short, the objection under discussion here is not really fatal to evolutionary procedure as such, but only to a misuse of it.

(3) A third objection to evolutionary sociology, and one perhaps on which greatest stress is laid in recent literature, is that it implies a unilinear or rectilinear order of development which is in plain contradiction with established fact. By unilinear development is meant that, both in regard to single institutions and complexes of institutions, all peoples have passed through a definite and unvarying sequence of stages. I do not know whether the 'classical evolutionists' ever really held such a preposterous doctrine. The biological analogy of the evolution of species certainly does not suggest a linear descent of cultural elements or entire cultures, but an enormously complicated divergent

growth along innumerable lines from a common source or common sources.[1] The briefest inspection of the facts of social evolution disposes of the notion of linear and uniform development. The forms of rigid monogamy, for example, which we find amongst some peoples of the lowest grades of culture, e.g. the Veddas or the Semang, cannot have been arrived at by a process at all analogous to that which established this system in medieval Europe. Again, we can distinguish in religious evolution a drift to monism either theistic or pantheistic. But the road which led to Hebrew monotheism is very different from that which led to monotheism of the Greeks, while the co-operation and synthesis of both was involved in the growth of the forms of monotheism which we find in Christianity. Other examples will readily occur to every one. It is clear that there is no single order of development, nor can any given form of an institution be invariably correlated with a determinate stage or phase of culture taken as a whole. But these facts are not merely clearly recognized but insisted upon by those who use the notion of evolution or development in sociology. A few citations may here be given. Müller-Lyer says explicitly that development is not in a single line and ' should be compared not to the upright trunk of the pine-tree, but rather to those leafy shrubs which produce several stems more or less directly rising from the same root

[1] In recent biology polyphyletic development is insisted on to a growing extent. Speaking of Botany, Prof. Bower says : ' It has been graphically stated that the present view of the lines of descent for vascular plants is more like a bundle of sticks than a connected tree ' (*Evolution in the Light of Modern Knowledge*, p. 167). In the animal world it has even been held that every species of metazoon has developed independently of all the others from a distinct species of protozoon (cf. Prof. Przibram, as quoted by Dr. W. T. Calman in his presidential address to Sec. D. of the B.A., 1930 : *Nature*, September 6th 1930).

and which subdivide into branches and twigs '.[1] It is moreover an essential part of his teaching that the development of cultures does not proceed entirely from within but depends upon stimulation from without, and the contact of different cultures. Hobhouse, in whose sociology the notion of development is central, points out that ' if human history grows towards a unity, its roots are in diversity, and down to our own time its advance is not simple and unitary but proceeds in many centres, none wholly independent, none without self-propulsion and idiosyncrasy '.[2] Tylor himself explained, in dealing with the evolution of religion, that the particular order of succession which he formulated was a minor matter. He was concerned to show rather that there was an essential continuity in the history of religion, ' that there seems no human thought so primitive as to have lost its bearing on our thought, nor so ancient as to have broken its connexion with our life '.[3] Jevons, again, who is often quoted as an example of classical evolutionism, plainly asserts that in his view evolution is not rectilinear but—to use Bergson's phrase—dispersive, that is, from a common starting-point many lines of evolution radiate in different directions.[4] In attacking unilinear development, the opponents of evolutionary sociology are, it seems to me, attacking a doctrine not now seriously entertained by any one, if it ever has been. But, it will be argued, the use of the comparative method in which instances are examined and correlated which are derived from different peoples and periods implies a uniform order of development. This is frequently asserted, but, as it seems to me, on insufficient grounds. In essence, the comparative

[1] *Phasen der Kultur*, English translation, p. 321.
[2] *Development and Purpose*, p. 190.
[3] cf. *Primitive Culture*, Vol. II, p. 452.
[4] cf. *Recent Developments in European Thought*, ed. Marvin, p. 80.

method is simply an application of the general rule of method to vary the circumstances of a phenomenon in order the better to discover its causes. With this object in view the comparative student of institutions utilizes information derived from the life of different peoples and ages.[1] In actual fact, the comparative method has frequently been combined with a method of explanation which consists in reconstructing the antecedents of a phenomenon and giving its history. But the use of the comparative method and explanation in genetic terms are by no means necessarily related. Prof. Westermarck, for example, pays very little attention to stages or phases of growth, but uses the comparative method throughout as an aid in disentangling the motives of institutions.[2] The comparative method may suggest genetic affinities, but need not do so. The method is also extremely important in the study of the interrelations between different social phenomena. The frequency with which different customs appear concurrently among different peoples may reveal an inner connexion between them which might have remained unrecognized if the association was noted only in a single group. This is the method of tracing 'adhesions' which Tylor formulated and applied to the institutions of marriage.[3] In this connexion, again, the method is independent of chronological sequences, though of course it may suggest them. Whatever view be taken of the nature of the comparative method, it is, I think, important to insist upon the necessity of not confusing morphology with history. The analogy of biology is here instructive. The danger of inferring common descent merely on the ground of morphological similarity has frequently been pointed out in recent

[1] cf. Joseph, *An Introduction to Logic*, p. 552.
[2] cf. his study of the practice of human sacrifice, *Moral Ideas*, Vol. I, p. 440 seq.
[3] cf. *Jour. Anthrop. Inst.*, 1889.

biological literature. Systematic classification should not be allowed to take the place of the direct tracing of phylogenesis either in sociology or biology.[1] It should be remembered, however, that in dealing with institutions of different peoples there is often direct evidence of historical connexion of a kind which compares favourably with the speculative genealogical schemes not infrequently employed in biology. I conclude that morphological classification, whether by the comparative method or otherwise, does not necessarily imply a unilinear order of development, and, since this notion is now explicitly repudiated by evolutionists, it seems that in this connexion again the polemic against the idea of evolution is, to put it mildly, misdirected.

(4) Somewhat similar considerations apply to a further objection to the use of evolutionary concepts in the study of culture which is urged by the ' Diffusionist ' or ' Historical ' school. It is clear that the existence of diffusion is fatal to the notion of an unvarying order of stages through which all peoples are supposed to pass, since, by the appropriation of cultural elements from alien sources, any people may occasionally make enormous leaps and so omit the intermediate stages. Objections of this kind have long been familiar. In England they were first made by Maitland.[2] In Germany the historical school (Graebner, Pater Schmidt, and others) is concerned to trace out the historical succession of what they term *Kultur-Kreise*, or complexes of culture traits, and their diffusion throughout the world. It is not generally noted, however, that independently of these schools Tarde long ago used his theory of ' imitation ' as a weapon against unilinear evolutionism. He pointed out with great vigour that legal systems, for

[1] *Morphologie und Historie müssen sich erst selbst ausweisen*; cf. Schaxel, *Grundzüge der Theorienbildung in der Biologie*, p. 43.

[2] cf. *Collected Papers*, Vol. III, pp. 285–303.

example, if left to themselves, show no tendency to evolve, but rather to remain stationary, and that such changes as do occur are due to the impact of external influences leading to imitation or fusion. He argued further that most legal systems had multiple origins and that their fluidity and continuity of transition were merely apparent. Like Professor Elliot Smith (but independently ?) he characterizes the opposed view as a belief in spontaneous generation.[1] Now arguments of this sort are conclusive against the notion of independent evolution occurring in different peoples in accordance with an unvarying order, a notion which, I take it, no one now wishes to defend. Have they any bearing on evolution in a wider sense ? One of the most outstanding representatives of 'classical evolutionism'—Tylor—explicitly asserts that, in accounting for any particular element of culture, 'three ways are open : independent invention, inheritance from ancestors in a distant region, and transmission from one race to another',[2] and he proceeds to offer some very judicious advice as to the best methods for deciding between these possibilities. It is clear that he took these different modes of growth as alternatives within the general framework of evolution, and in this he was clearly right. We may get some light on this problem by considering the very similar questions that arise in biology. There, too, we meet with cases of what is called parallel evolution. Darwin himself considered parallel variations and ascribed them to the action of unknown causes upon a similar constitution, or to the reappearance of characters possessed by a more or less remote ancestor. In recent biology the evidence for homologous variations has accumulated both for plants and animals, and the notion of what is termed homoplastic

[1] cf. *Les Transformations du Droit*, 1894, Bk. VII.
[2] cf. *Early History of Mankind*, p. 374.

evolution has been more and more widely extended.[1] No one, I take it, would regard these cases of parallel evolution as contradictory of the general theory of evolution, though they have a bearing upon the problem of polygenesis as against monogenesis, and also perhaps upon the existence of directive tendencies within the race determining parallel but independent variations in the same direction.[2] Another biological analogy, which has a bearing upon the problem of diffusion, is suggested by recent discussions of the part played by race-crossing in the creation of new forms. The balance of opinion seems to be that race-crossing does not in itself produce genuine mutations but may, in favourable circumstances, lead to the establishment and perpetuation of 'combinations' of traits derived from different sources.[3] That 'hybridization' is important in social evolution there can be no question. There are innumerable instances of social changes produced by the clash and contact of different cultural elements, or of the sudden release of pent-up forces as the result of stimuli from without.[4]

Bearing these considerations in mind, we may formulate the problems that arise in connexion with diffusion thus: Given similarities in culture in different parts of the world, they may be (i) due to independent evolution, (ii) they may be parallel but independent developments expressing what may be called a common phyletic

[1] cf. Tansley, B.A. Report, 1923, p. 246. An interesting case in connexion with our problem may be quoted from Wheeler, who shows that social habits of ants, bees, and wasps have been acquired independently for each, and probably more than once in some of the three groups.

[2] cf. Bower, *The Ferns*, p. 293.

[3] cf. Alverdes, *Rassen und Artbildung*, VI.

[4] A great historian of religion has gone so far as to say that there never has been any religious development except when different religions have come into contact with one another (cf. Tiele, *Elements of the Science of Religion*, Vol. I, p. 236).

drift, (iii) they may be due to diffusion, (iv) they may be due to 'convergent' evolution from originally different sources, (v) the parallels may not be genuine but merely apparent.[1] Another set of problems arises when diffusion does not result in the mere acceptance of alien cultural elements, but results in new formations in which the borrowed elements are transformed, or possibly a new trend of development is stimulated, as the result of the contact. All these questions fall within the general framework of the evolutionary theory. It is thus clear that diffusion cannot be contrasted with evolution or identified with it: rather is it one of the agencies of evolution serving either as a mechanism of transmission or, especially in the case of non-material elements of culture which are rarely transmitted unmodified, also of variation and growth.

(5) I come now to a further objection to the use of

[1] An example of independent evolution is offered by the history of bronze, which, according to Kroeber (*Anthropology*, p. 228), was developed independently, and later in the Western hemisphere than in the Eastern. The second type of cases may be easily illustrated from the history of language. For example, the English type of plural represented by foot, feet; mouse, mice, is strictly parallel with the German Fuss, Füsse; Maus, Maüse. But these changes took place at different periods in German and English, and are referred back to 'some general tendency or group of tendencies at work in early Germanic long before English and German had developed as such, that eventually drove both these dialects along closely parallel paths' Sapir, *Language*, p. 185). An example of (iii) is the spread of the alphabet, but of course there are innumerable others. Good instances of convergent growth are again furnished by languages. Thus the drift towards the loss of formal mechanisms, and towards the expression of grammar by material elements and their position only, can be illustrated from the history of the Indo-European languages, Chinese, and Polynesian. A comparable phenomenon is perhaps the growth of feudalism in China a thousand years earlier than in Europe, or the growth of an empire in Peru structurally similar to the empires of the Orient. (cf. Kroeber, *Anthropology*, p. 125). For spurious parallels, see thei nteresting discussion in R. B. Dixon, *The Building of Cultures*, Chap. VI. On the whole question cf. F. v. Luschan, *Zusammenhänge und Konvergenz*, 1918.

evolutionary concepts in sociology with which I have the greatest sympathy, though, as will be seen, it is valid only against an exclusively biological interpretation of human history rather than as against the general idea of human development. The use of biological analogies has led many people to assume that the causes which operate in biological evolution are also those which account for the phenomena of cultural development. Hence, for example, the appeal to natural selection, the tendency to explain historical processes by reference to racial qualities, and the like. Obviously, this is much too large a subject for adequate discussion here. I will confine myself to a few observations which arise naturally in connexion with the arguments discussed under our previous heads. I should like to urge that, if there is evolution in social change, the processes involved differ entirely from those which constitute biological evolution, and that to appeal to biology is to seek to explain the better known in terms of the less known. For the historic period it has proved methodologically hopeless to establish any correlation between forms of culture and race groupings. It is obvious that races are too mixed and cultures too intertwined to enable us to refer specific cultural elements to specific racial elements. Even for the prehistoric period, when race mixture had not proceeded so far, efforts to establish any correlation between forms of culture and forms of race grouping have up to now failed.[1] Such failure, it must be granted, is only negative evidence, since it may be due not to absence of correlation but to deficiency in methods of investigation. There are, however, other considerations which strongly suggest that racial change and social change differ in character and method. Firstly, the rate of

[1] cf. The Appendix, by Dr. E. Wahle, in W. Scheidt, *Allgemeine Rassenkunde*, Vol. I, p. 563.

social change is such that it cannot possibly be attributed to changes in germinal structure, for which there is no independent evidence for the historic period and which, in any case, would be much too slow to account for the vast social changes that have occurred. Moreover, it is extremely unlikely that any of the eras in which striking advances were made were due to, or accompanied by, changes in the inherited constitution of man. As Galton pointed out,[1] they must be referred rather to a new orientation given to human faculty, principally, it would seem, caused by contact with new or strange cultures. It seems probable also that the proportion of gifted men produced is fairly constant, while the expression or realization of their potentialities awaits and depends upon opportunities provided by the occasions of exceptional stir and exhilaration present in the epochs of progress.[2] When culture contact occurs, there may also be race contact or fusion. Accordingly, many writers have found in this fresh arguments for emphasizing the purely biological agencies on the ground that the really vital factor in such circumstances is the invigorating effect of new blood. It is clear, however, that, in a great many instances at any rate, culture contact results in vast changes where the purely ethnic effects are slight or nil. I will mention a few. The megalithic culture, to which so much importance is attached now by some theorists, was only in a minor degree the result of a racial drift.[3] The so-called Aryan conquest in India, according to Crooke, was more a moral and an intellectual one than a substitution of the white man for the dark-skinned people. The ethnogenic effects of the Roman conquest in France,

[1] cf. *Enquiry into Human Faculty*, p. 129.
[2] For an interesting discussion on this point, cf. Balfour, *Decadence*, pp. 59–62.
[3] cf. Gordon Childe, *The Aryans*, p. 156.

according to Pittard, was *quasiment nulle.*[1] The Norman Conquest, according to Haddon, did not modify the physical type of England and Wales. In our own time the effects of the contact between white and coloured peoples are out of proportion to the degree of racial admixture. It thus seems likely that, even where there is physical admixture, what is really important is the stimulus that culture contact, which comes with it, provides. In any event we know so little about racial differences in mental characters that to use them as a basis of historical explanation is certainly a leap in the dark. Such explanation is in many instances flagrantly circular. We infer the race qualities from the culture, and then turn round and explain the culture by the race qualities.

In general, it seems to me, the present position of biology in regard to all the major issues is too uncertain to afford much help to the sociologist. Thus, for example, practically nothing is known of the origin of variations, and the bearing of such mutations as have been studied by modern Geneticists upon evolution is much disputed. We may in this connexion quote the authoritative statement of Johannsen: 'Dagegen sind jetzt viele Beispiele von Mutationen bekannt, sowie auch von genotypischen Neukonbinationen nach Kreuzung. Alle diese diskontinuierlichen "Typenänderungen" mögen ein gewisses prinzipielles Interesse für die Deszendenzlehre haben. Jedoch sind alle diese Änderungen so klein, dass sie kaum ein direktes Interesse für das Verständnis der grösseren Züge einer Evolution beanspruchen können.'[2] I do not think we are in such a desperate position in regard to social changes. In human life teleological factors are plainly operative; changes are

[1] cf. *Les Races et L'Histoire*, p. 157.

[2] cf. *Allgemeine Biologie*, 'Kultur der Gegenwart', Part III, p. 659.

brought about by a process of trial and error or by deliberate effort directed towards ends more or less clearly apprehended. Again, nothing is more certain than that in social history vast changes are brought about by the accumulation of small differences. This has long been recognized in dealing with the evolution of artifacts, but is equally clear in the changes which take place in law and custom. There is no mystery about the process at all, for here, of course, the evolution is the result of co-operative and cumulative experience whereby those who come later benefit by the achievements of their predecessors. In biology, on the other hand, the formation of species by the accumulation of small modifications is extraordinarily difficult to understand and by many biologists is denied.[1] Further, one of the outstanding difficulties of biological theory is how to account for the appearance of correlated structural changes in dealing, for example, with the evolution of such complex organs as the eye.[2] There is no such difficulty in dealing with social changes; not only does one idea, for example, suggest another to the same individual, but, as the history of science and invention shows, a great deal is due to the co-operation of different minds. The process of invention is consciously directed, and in any case is ready to seize upon discoveries accidentally made in the course of investigation or otherwise. To the biologist, again, the survival and spread of mutants presents a difficult problem, while in sociology recourse may be had readily to the mechanisms of imitation and embodiment in tradition. Moreover, while mutations

[1] cf. Bateson's statement: 'The effect of Mendelian analysis is that we have to recognize now that the transferable characters do not culminate in specific distinctions and that these are not reached by the accumulation of small differences' (*Birkbeck Centenary Lectures*, pp. 121–5).

[2] cf. Bergson's remark: 'Il faut maintenant que toutes changent à la fois et que chacune consulte les autres' (*Évolution Créatrice*, p. 71).

are rare, inventions are fairly common, so that significant changes are produced rapidly and without involving any changes in the inherited structure. Finally, the problem of orthogenesis, or evolution in what appears a directed line, has so far remained insoluble in biology. Equal mystery surrounds the question of 'progressive' evolution. Thomson[1] suggests that progressiveness may be due to the fact that, as organisms develop, the whole web of life outside the organism becomes more complex and the interrelations more intricate. Accordingly, selection, operating as it does in relation to the environment, is bound to act progressively. But if, as seems generally agreed, selection does not in itself influence the direction of mutations, it is difficult to see why mutations should arise which necessarily fit into the more intricate environment. In social evolution, orthogenesis and progressive development are in better case. The effect of changes in the environment are here cumulative. Each new generation can start on the basis of what has been acquired by past generations, since the method of transmission does not depend upon physical heredity. We may say, in effect, that owing to this latter fact social evolution proceeds through the inheritance of 'acquired characters' in the sense that what has once been acquired is either directly transmitted or its acquisition is facilitated through the instrumentality of social institutions. In short, not only is social change totally different in character from biological change, but it is far more intelligible and not exposed to anything like the same extent to the difficulties which at present confront biological theory.

B.—I have now dealt with the most important criticisms that have been recently directed against the use of evolutionary ideas in sociology. While none of these are fatal, they do point to the need of an examination

[1] cf. *System of Animate Nature*, Vol. II, p. 468.

into what is meant by evolution, and into the nature of what it is that is supposed to evolve. To this I now turn.

The concept of evolution is notoriously ambiguous. A detailed analysis of the numerous senses in which it has been used is clearly out of place here. Perhaps, it will be agreed that, common to most views of evolution is that it is a process of change culminating in the production of something new but exhibiting an orderly continuity in transition. The notion that evolution is a movement from the simple to the complex can be, and has been, seriously disputed. There is apparently little ground for believing that the physical universe is an evolution from some pre-existing *simpler* order. As applied to institutions, it is by no means clear that primitive languages or systems of kinship, for example, are necessarily simpler than the more advanced ones. Further, there appears to be equally little agreement about other alleged 'formal' characters of evolution. There remains only the notion of novelty in continuity or continuity in novelty. The 'new' is said to be 'potentially' contained in the old, but the notion of the potential again is very vaguely used. As Bradley pointed out, it is often a mere attempt at a compromise between the 'is' and the 'is not'. Theories of evolution, in fact, hover between epigenesis and pre-formation. None the less, a meaning can perhaps be attached to the term potential which is helpful in characterizing evolution. A thing exists potentially when conditions are present which will lead to its occurrence providing certain other specifiable conditions are superadded. Not all the cause-factors of an occurrence can, however, be described as containing it potentially. Whether they can or not depends on their importance relatively to the superadded conditions which are necessary for the completed occurrence. The superadded conditions, in short, must not be of such high magnitude as to destroy the individuality of the thing, or to break its continuity.[1]

This requirement is sometimes expressed in the form that evolution implies the persistence of an identical subject or unchanging substance, and it is even argued that this must be timeless or supra-temporal. But I doubt whether evolution really carries with it such a vast implication. There must be something the same, it is true, throughout the process of development, and there must also be something new. We have here one form of the relation between permanence and change, but the difficulty seems to be capable of being resolved if it be remembered that permanence and change do not refer to self-sufficient entities, but are two aspects of concrete existence. The unity which belongs to a substance is a causal unity of connexion between its manifestations, and this, as Johnson has shown,[2] does not imply any qualitative or quantitative constancy. Johnson's treatment of the 'continuant' provides, I should like to suggest, a way of restating the problem of evolution. The continuant, as I understand it, is a series of manifestations linked by a unique relation which binds them into a whole or unity. This relation is conceived primarily as a particular type of causal connectedness, namely, that of immanent causality. He shows [3] that there are all degrees of unity in continuants according to the complexity of the relationship of immanent and transeunt interactions which they exhibit. If now we refer back to what was said above about potentialities we may, I suggest, describe evolution as a process in which the potentialities of a continuant are realized predominantly by way of immanent causality and to a relatively minor extent by way of transeunt

[1] cf. Bradley, *Appearance and Reality*, Chap. XXIV.
[2] *Logic*, III, Chap. VII, especially pp. 99–100.
[3] Ibid., p. 93.

causality. The superadded conditions which are necessary for the realization of the potentiality must, that is to say, be largely related to earlier phases of the continuant by way of immanent causality. No development is, of course, exclusively determined from within, since the continuant always needs an environment if it is to develop at all. What is meant is rather that the primary sources of change shall be referable to immanent forces.[1] If this view be accepted, it will be seen that the term evolution is in itself not explanatory. It merely asserts that there are immanent factors involved in the observed processes of change. Until the nature of these is known, and their relation to external factors ascertained, we have done very little in the way of explanation. The study of the various forms of development reveals two principal types; there is development of a continuant (or development *in* a unity) when, and in so far as, that continuant passes through a sequence of phases in the course of which (*a*) it, or rather its parts or characters, become more distinct or articulate though the whole is not less efficiently organized as a unity, or (*b*) the whole becomes more efficiently organized as a unity without loss of distinctness of its parts or characters. In general, traits or characters differentiate out of a unity in which they were at first merged or confounded so that we only identify then *ex post facto*. But secondly, there is also development *of* a unity which does not appear to exist in the beginning, by synthesis. Sexual reproduction is of this kind, and perhaps much of what is called emergent evolution. It is possible, however, that in development of this kind we must infer that before the synthesis the elements entering into it were really parts of a wider and more inclusive

[1] It may be noted in passing that the usual criteria of advance and the classification into 'higher' and 'lower' levels really express degrees of immanence or self-dependence.

continuant, so that they had a sort of fitness or predisposition to each other. Thus, for example, one may regard the evolution of species as the history of a racial continuant [1] of which individual organisms are sub-continuants. If this is so, then the second form of development may be really a case of the first.

If this account of the nature of evolution be accepted, the problem of evolution in sociology resolves itself into the question whether the history of human culture is a continuum within which changes occur in accordance with immanent causality. That in some sense elements of culture, such as language, religion, science, are continua possessed of a certain unity and an immanent nature, seems generally agreed. Thus, for example, languages are regarded as wholes having a definite structure or configuration. They tend to persist and maintain an equilibrium which, if disturbed at any point, is corrected by supplementary changes often spread over centuries. They show, moreover, determinate drifts having definite direction and resulting in a continual readjustment of the patterned equilibrium. Further, the changes which languages undergo cannot at present be explained entirely in terms of random individual variations, and their direction can only be inferred from the past history of the given language.[2] So, again, science has an inner unity and its growth is not one of mere accretion but of assimilation and inward transformation. 'La science,' says Prof. Abel Rey, 'c'est ensuite une société d'organismes vivants qui, comme tous les organismes, gardent, au-dessous des changements qui marquent leur croissance, cette individualité cachée qui en fait un organisme. . . . Rien là d'une évolution en mosaïque. Mais une continuité en profondeur.' [3] Of religion, Prof. Jevons says,

[1] cf. Hertwig's conception of a *Lebensprozess der Art.*
[2] cf. Sapir, *Language*, pp. 165–6.
[3] *La Science Orientale avant les Grecs*, p. 13.

'If evolution takes place, something must be evolved and that something, as being continuously present in all the different stages may be called the continuum of religion.'[1] These remarks suggest that if evolution is rightly applicable to social changes, the subjects of evolution are cultures or elements of cultures, but this would be seriously misleading. Languages or religions, for example, are not entities evolving independently of men in pursuit of their own ends. The real subjects undergoing development are men in societies who speak and think and are religious. It is only for convenience of study that we speak of the evolution of cultural elements. In truth, the evolution of language, or of religion, or of morality, is only an aspect of the evolution of society, and it is because of this fact that the growth of each can only be understood if considered in relation to that of the rest. It remains that the continuity of cultural evolution suggests that, in a sense, societies and possibly mankind as a whole are true continuants, and it is this which, as it seems to me, is really required to make the application of the notion of evolution intelligible.

To carry the argument further it is necessary to show that the changes which societies undergo are the expression of factors immanent in them as wholes. This is seriously disputed by many philosophers. Driesch,[2] for example, argues that in history there is only cumulation, that is, systems are formed by additions and interactions, but there is no evolution in the strict sense, which, according to him, implies control by an inner or organic principle. He does not deny that there is, in some sense, an historical whole, but insists that this whole has no dynamic value, and that the moving agents are always individuals, perhaps only a very few individuals. Driesch's refusal to admit evolution in history seems,

[1] cf. *Introduction to the History of Religion*, p. 8.
[2] *Geist und Gesellschaft*, p. 19.

however, to be based on his assumption that there is only evolution when there is an *überpersönliches Ens* guiding and animating the entire process. But, as I have argued above, the notion of evolution does not necessarily imply a persistent subject in the sense of a super-personal entelechy, but is applicable to continuants undergoing change in accordance with immanent causality. The real question seems to be whether all that occurs in the history of societies is, or ultimately will turn out to be, explicable in terms of transeunt causality between their parts. Now, in a paper I read to this Society some years ago,[1] I argued that societies are essentially conational unities, that is, wholes which maintain themselves as such by the efforts of their parts to mutual adjustment. If such be the nature of societies, it would seem that the laws governing their life will be (*a*) those of the human mind, (*b*) those of the interactions between minds, (*c*) those of the cumulative consequences of such interactions. It follows that in a sense it is true that the sources of social change are to be found in individual minds and that, as Driesch says, *Der Einzelne ist stäts der Täter*. Yet the individual can only set before himself ends which are immanent or inherent in human nature, and though social events are made up of complex interactions between individuals and thus appear to be explicable in terms of transeunt relations between them, yet these causes could only take effect if it were part of the nature of individuals to respond to mutual stimulus and to find satisfaction in ends socially conditioned and common to the unitary whole of which they are members. In this sense, may we not say, with Tiele, 'The history of men is at the same time the history of humanity'?[2]

At this point the question will be raised whether, even

[1] See Chapter III, pp. 49 seq.

[2] cf. *Elements of the Science of Religion*, p. 264.

if it be granted that societies or communities are continuants and exhibit a sort of conational unity, the same is true of humanity or mankind. Is not the lesson of history that of indifference, dispersion, conflict ? And if mankind has no unity, how can it be said to be undergoing development ? That there is no unilinear development is clear, as we have already seen. It may be granted further that we are apt, as Troeltsch has argued, with great vigour, to set up Western or European-American civilization as a standard and to identify its development with the development of humanity. The ideal of humanity, Troeltsch urges, is only disguised European arrogance. 'Palestine, Rome, Wittenberg, and Geneva are the centres of the earth, and from them comes the only flock with its only shepherd, the realm of absolute truth and salvation of which the modern equivalent is the realm of the only culture, wisdom, and science. The conqueror, the colonizer, the missionary, lurk behind all European thought. This is the source of its practical efficiency and power, but also of much error and exaggeration.'[1] That there is much justice in these remarks cannot be denied. Nothing is more common in the philosophy of history than to regard the line followed by the European peoples as the main highway of history, and to measure all other civilizations by the degree to which they approximate or have contributed to European civilization. Yet Troeltsch's arguments are surely insufficient to justify his conclusion that the unity of mankind is but 'a metaphysical fairy-tale told of a non-existing entity'. To begin with, there is abundant evidence to show that some interconnexion there always has been between human groups. Even the simplest communities which have been studied by anthropologists have been influenced by contact with their neighbours. The Bushmen of South Africa have learnt from the

[1] cf. Schmoller's *Jahrbuch*, 1920, p. 6.

Negro; the Eskimo has learnt from the Indian; the Negrito from the Malay; the Veddah from the Singhalese.[1] Recent archaeological work brings out the fundamental continuity of the Oriental world. Egyptian, Babylonian, and Indian civilizations had a common basis and regular intercourse, the connexion of European civilizations with those of the Orient is conclusively established, and the lines of their propagation are being mapped out with increasing clearness. Moreover, the evolution of cultural elements in the sense of descent with modifications is in many respects more clearly and securely established than is descent in biology.[2] The clearest case is the evolution of language. The tendency of recent studies in comparative philology has been, I understand, to establish connexions between linguistic stocks which had formerly appeared to be very remote from each other,[3] and their derivation from a common source seems not improbable. In the sphere of material culture the continuity of growth is most obvious. Metallurgy is a most striking instance of this interdependence, and there is positive evidence of the continuity of tradition relating to it, though its original cradle may be hard to identify. Similarly there seems to be some unity behind the traits usually brought together under the heading of Neolithic culture.[4] Again, in religion, genealogical affinities and mutual interaction have been established in many instances, though here, as in other elements of culture, it is necessary to distinguish between genuine assimilative growth and mere syncretism.

To sum up, a survey of culture suggests that while

[1] cf. Boas, *Anthropology and Modern Life*, p. 209.

[2] cf. Tylor, *Primitive Culture*, I, Chap. I.

[3] cf. Meillet, *Les Langues dans l'Europe Nouvelle*, p. 61. It may be noted that Darwin himself used the case of language to illustrate the principle of genealogical classification (*Origin*, p. 578).

[4] cf. Gordon Childe, *The Most Ancient East*, pp. 225–8.

specific cultures follow their own course and have an immanent nature of their own, they are yet interdependent and contribute to the main stream of the history of humanity. There is such a thing as science, and not merely the sciences of different peoples and ages; religion, and not merely religions; civilization, and not merely civilizations. The highest achievements of mankind are perhaps also the most enduring, and in the long run the most pervasive. The convergence of the higher religious and moral systems to a common point is especially noteworthy, and may be regarded as perhaps the most important evidence of the development of humanity. Finally, if there always has been some unity and interconnexion in the historical process, there can be no doubt that this unity itself has undergone development. By a series of synthesis, organization has extended and increasingly inclusive vital continuants have been formed. Above all, men have become increasingly conscious of a fundamental unity of purpose and a good common to all mankind. It is perhaps not too optimistic to hope that eventually the interdependent vital orders which we call nations and peoples will find the forms of organization requisite for the realization of their common ideals and aspirations. If the idea of a unitary mankind and of human development is itself a product of history, is it not deeply rooted in the needs of men, and does it not point to an underlying or immanent drive behind the intricate and painful efforts at unification which we see in history? We have seen above that the term development is used in two senses: there is development *in* a unity, and development, through synthesis, *of* a unity, and it was suggested that the latter form is possibly a case of the former. In the history of humanity both forms of development seem to have taken place. In all the larger elements of culture, processes of differentiation and integration have been traced by sociologists. Determinate drifts of great depth and continuity have been shown to characterize the large-scale movements of religion, science, and morals. In all these synthesis or hybridization has played an important part, and with increasing synthesis has come a gradual realization of the essential unity of aim and purpose binding all mankind. That, to a large extent, this vast process of correlated growth can be interpreted in terms of cumulative interaction between individuals is probable. But if individuals make society, it is equally true that society makes individuals. Social continuants are then genuine, possibly emergent, wholes. Their formation and interweaving into the wider and more inclusive continuant of mankind is, it is claimed, an expression of agencies immanent in the entire process of history. The latter may accordingly be described as the self-forming of humanity. This is what seems to be implied in the use of evolutionary concepts in sociology.

V

A NOTE ON THE CONCEPTION OF STAGES IN SOCIAL EVOLUTION

IT is proposed in this paper to discuss in outline the various ways in which the conception of stages or phases has been used in anthropology and sociology and to inquire whether, and in what sense, it still has value as an instrument of investigation. We may distinguish five ways in which the notion of stages has been employed, having different roots in the history of thought and, as will appear later, possessed of very unequal value for sociological theory. There is, first of all, the notion of stages as regular sequences of some element or form of culture, such as forms of the family or economic organization, supposed to recur in the same order among different peoples and to describe a kind of evolutionary tendency. This may be described as the conception of unilinear recurrence, and is connected with the early and somewhat crude application of evolutionary ideas to sociological problems. There is, secondly, the notion of stages as describing general trends of social development in humanity or rather in the culture of humanity, taken as a whole. This view has its roots partly in modern evolutionary ideas, but more profoundly in older conceptions of development derived from the philosophy of history and general philosophical theory. The notion of recurrence or orderly repetition of given sequences of stages does not on this view play an important rôle. It is recognized that development proceeds on different lines and reaches focal points of expression in different parts of the world. What it stresses rather is the interconnexion and continuity of human history, and the possibility of detecting in it general trends characteristic of human culture as a whole. Examples are the schemes of development formulated by Comte, Hegel, Marx, Hobhouse. Thirdly, there are the less ambitious schemes of those who formulate schemes of change for one or more elements of culture, but confine themselves, at any rate primarily, to the history of one people or culture area, though no doubt leaving open the possibility of parallel schemes being found to apply also to other peoples or areas. Compare here Schmoller's [1] scheme of stages describing the economic growth of Germany, or the scheme of Proesler [2] more deliberately restricted to Germany. In most of the schemes coming under the heads so far mentioned there is implied the notion of genetic continuity, that is, subsequent stages are held to arise or evolve out of precedent stages. The fourth point of view is to leave the question of genetic continuity open and to regard the stages distinguished not as descriptive of sequences supposed to have actually occurred but rather as heuristic constructions or theoretical 'types' useful as instruments of measurement, comparison, and correlation. Here belongs the notion of 'ideal types' used by Max Weber [3] and adopted by even the severest critic of the theory of stages in general such as von Below.[4] Finally there is the theory of *Kultur-Kreise*, or culture complexes, according to which social development consists in the stratification or superposition of different complexes of cultural elements, their fusion and mutual modification through migration or other contacts in the course of time.[5]

[1] *Grundriss der allgemeinen Volkwirtschaftslehre.*
[2] *Die Epochen der deutschen Wirtschaftsentwicklung.*
[3] *Gesammelte Aufsätze zur Wissenschaftslehre.*
[4] *Probleme der Wirtschaftsgeschichte.*
[5] cf. the works of Graebner and P. Schmidt.

A detailed examination of the numerous inquiries included under these five modes of procedure would require, and perhaps justify, a lengthy volume. Here I must confine myself to a somewhat summary evaluation. The first type of theory, namely, that of unilinear recurrence, has been subjected to much criticism and is now perhaps hardly held by any one. The sequence, for example, of 'hunting, pastoral, agricultural', often put forward by earlier writers, has been shown by ethnologists to be quite unfounded. Pastoral nomadism never developed for obvious geographical reasons in the South Sea Islands, nor has it existed in America, where agriculture grew up side by side with hunting and did not pass through the supposedly universal intermediate pastoral phase. Similarly, there is no reason for accepting any particular scheme of the forms of the family as judged by the number of the partners (monogamy, polygamy, polyandry, etc.) as universal, or to hold that mankind everywhere passed from a stage of mother-right to one of father-right. Instances could be multiplied from other spheres of social evolution to show the falsity of any hypothesis of uniform repetition of sequences in different parts of the world.

Despite the admitted failure of these earlier schemes it would be a mistake to regard them as having been useless, or even to conclude that the problems which they were intended to solve have been satisfactorily disposed of. They have undoubtedly revealed the existence of deep-seated parallel or common elements in the cultures of different peoples, as, for example, in the sphere of mythology [1] or in religion.[2] Some, but by no means all, the earlier writers erred in not paying sufficient attention to the influence of contact between different peoples and to the phenomena of borrowing

[1] Ehrenreich, P.: *Die allgemeine Mythologie.*
[2] Otto, R.: *Religious Essays*, Chap. X.

and diffusion. They also seem to have assumed far too readily that the stages they distinguished were genetically connected in the sense that each stage necessarily or automatically gave rise to a subsequent one. In doing so they failed to take account of diffusion or of the possibility of convergent evolution from sources originally different and by stages not necessarily similar. The problems suggested by the occurrence of parallel development remain, and it is conceivable that further analysis and comparative study may yet succeed in the formulation of trends of development immanent in the human race, though not necessarily capable of being expressed in the crude form of sequences artificially contrived for purposes of provisional classification—trends possibly masked by the occurrence of deviations due to variations in geographical conditions, or to the subtle and infinitely interwoven relationships and interactions of social evolution.

Any attempt to deal with the schemes included in the second group with the brevity here necessary must be very difficult and may be thought presumptuous. I will confine myself to an enumeration of their chief characteristics and to a brief statement of their standing in the present stage of knowledge. They have certain characteristics in common which may be first mentioned. (i) They seek to formulate the general trends of human evolution and are not primarily interested in the question whether the processes they describe are necessarily repeated in the same order in different periods of time, or among different peoples. (ii) They are schemes of correlated growth linking up the various elements of culture between which they see essential interrelations. (iii) They suggest a theory of the causes underlying the historical process, of which they show a much richer insight than do the schemes hitherto discussed. Hegel's conception of social development as a series of processes through which there takes place an expansion of the area of freedom is generally regarded as seizing something essential in, at any rate European, history, and his description of the dialectical movement of thought has drawn attention to the numerous instances of changes occurring by way of action and re-action in the history of thought and speculation as well as in other movements in social life. Comte's law of three stages, though it can be criticized in the light of our better knowledge of primitive mentality and also of later thought, is generally admitted as summing up in a fruitful and suggestive way at least certain aspects of the movement of thought.[1] Whatever estimate may be formed of the value of the Marxian theory, its heuristic importance cannot be doubted, and it has in fact affected recent workers in history and sociology profoundly. Hobhouse's synthesis[2] differs from all the others in being based on a very comprehensive survey of the data of anthropology and history and on the facts of comparative psychology. Without attempting any examination of these ambitious theories, I wish to urge that syntheses of the kind sought by them must be the goal of sociological inquiry, if sociology is ever to go beyond the mere compilation of data. Comte and Hegel have been criticized on the ground that they concentrate too much on European history, and that they tend to regard the European civilizations as the standard by which all the other civilizations are to be measured. In this criticism there is some justice, but the limitation censured was inevitable at the time when Hegel and Comte were writing. A more fundamental objection is that made familiar by Troeltsch[3] and his followers, who urge that there can be no such thing as a history of humanity

[1] Hobhouse, L. T. *The Law of the Three Stages.* (*Soc. Rev.*, 1908.)
[2] *Social Development.*
[3] *Der Historismus und seine Probleme.*

as a whole. There seem to be two points in Troeltsch's argument which require to be distinguished. One is that with regard to other culture areas, with the exception perhaps of the Islamic, we do not possess the necessary historical material of the scientific nature required by the European historian. This, of course, is true, and the remedy can be found, if at all, in more intensive preparatory studies by Europeans and still more by scholars native to the areas in question. The second point is far more fundamental. Universal history is impossible, for humanity has no unity and cannot be studied as a whole. Any attempt at a universal history that goes beyond mere *Buchbinder-synthese* which brings together in one volume distinct histories of numerous peoples, results either in a vague romantic contemplation and falls a prey in the end to a relativistic scepticism, as in the case of Spengler, or else results in a tacit application of European standards to the whole world, as in the case of H. G. Wells, 'the characteristic Anglo-Saxon counterpart to the German romantic, Spengler'. Yet Troeltsch does not deny the importance of sociological, as distinct from historical, attempts at drawing up schemes of development for the whole of mankind, and speaks with approval of the efforts of Breysig, Vierkandt, and Max Weber. His further argument that European culture is a unique product in which numerous lines of development converge and fuse into a new whole, does not affect the value of a study devoted to an analysis of the various factors involved, and in such an analysis a study of forms of contact and resulting syntheses of cultures elsewhere must manifestly be of assistance even to the student of European history.

To my third group belong those schemes of social evolution which avoid the assumption of unilinear recurrence, and in many cases are frankly designed as descriptive of a single culture only. They are very numerous. For economic stages alone Proesler in his survey enumerates about fifty schemes. If schemes dealing with all aspects of culture were included, such as mythology, religion, forms of government, the list would be probably more than doubled. Here I must confine myself to a brief statement—somewhat dogmatic I fear—of the conclusions relating to method which a survey of these numerous schemes has suggested to me:

1. In dealing with the simpler peoples the chief mistake made by theorists has been to lump them all together as though they belonged to one level. There is need for an agreed classification at any rate on the basis of the economic level attained by the various peoples.

2. Despite formal repudiation of any belief in unilinear recurrence writers often unconsciously tend to extend their particular sequence of stages to other areas or cultures.

3. Care should be taken to avoid question-begging assumptions of causal relationship in choosing the characters which are to form the basis of classification. Thus, for example, economic stages are often distinguished on the basis of the degree of social differentiation or political structure, thus implying a necessary relation between them. This may easily lead to error. A good example of this is Schmoller's category of Territorial Economy (sixteenth to eighteenth centuries). Below [1] shows that the growth of territorial States did not fundamentally alter the economic order which could still be adequately described by Bücher's category of Town Economy.

4. There is great need of schemes deliberately restricted to single culture areas after the manner

[1] *Probleme der Wirtschaftsgeschichte*, Chap. VIII.

of Proesler's work on the economic development of Germany.[1] If such schemes were worked out by specialists for other countries, and not only for economic, but also for other aspects of culture, the correlating work of the sociologist would be facilitated and put on a securer basis.

5. For some aspects of culture, notably religion and morals, and possibly law, the data are already so vast that a concerted effort might well be made now to work out comparable schemes of development for the different civilizations.

Before dealing further with the problems involved I will give a brief account of the fourth way of conceiving stages, namely, that connected with the theory of Ideal Types worked out by Weber and others. Weber recognizes that in dealing with the entities of sociology and history, such as the State or Christianity, we cannot hope to seize, and embody in a set of words, the infinite complexity and variety of the phenomena which are intended to be conveyed by the terms. We are bound to use what he calls 'ideal types' and which are perhaps better described as heuristic constructions. They are not definitions nor averages. They are rather constructions which we arrive at by intensifying or emphasizing certain characteristics of a group of occurrences, and by linking up with them others which perhaps are not always found in association or do not always take place in the same way, but are so combined by us as to form a coherent or unitary whole. Thus in working with the notion of medieval Christianity we do not attempt to gather together the infinitely varied and even contradictory beliefs, feelings, and forms of behaviour of an endless number of individuals of a given time. We construct a scheme which is what may be described as a limiting concept, including certain

[1] Proesler, *Die Epochen der deutschen Wirtschaftsentwicklung.*

dogmatic beliefs, moral ideas, and maxims of conduct, which we weave into a whole and with which we compare the actual reality. No doubt the elements which we use in our constructions are all derived from experience, and we bring them together in accordance with our notion of what is objectively possible. But the scheme is confessedly relative, an instrument for measurement and comparison and not supposed to be exemplified empirically in its pure form. This notion of ideal types is applied by Weber to individual historical entities (in Rickert's sense), but, as he shows, it can also be used in the study of development. We may, in other words, construct an ideal series by taking into consideration objective possibilities of growth and then use the series as a measure of the actual historical happenings which also then form a test of the validity of our construction. Thus, for example, if we start with the ideal type of a handicraft economy, we deduce that in a society so organized, the only source of capital accumulation is to be found in ground rent. We then infer that the factors leading to a transformation of the system would be found in a limited supply of land, an increase of the population, an influx of precious metals, and an increasing rationalization of conduct or behaviour. We then compare our deductions with the actual facts, and if they do not correspond we can infer that the society with which we started was not based exclusively on handicraft, and we are led to a deeper investigation. In Weber's view the so-called laws of evolution are such constructions, and as such they are of great utility. They become misleading when they are regarded as empirically valid, or still worse, as forces. He thinks the Marxian formulae are of this nature and are heuristically important. They are thus admittedly relative, are bound to change with increasing knowledge, and are inevitable in the present early stage of the social sciences. It may be added that the severest critic of the notion of stages, von Below, readily admits the importance of this method of investigation.[1] Weber himself applied it with great success in his numerous studies, especially in his work on the various forms of domination or authority or in his study of the forms of towns, and it is important to note that a conclusion of the greatest significance emerges from his work, namely, the discovery of a general trend, the increasing rationalization of social life and culture.

We may now examine whether and in what sense the conception of stages has value in sociology. Sociology I take to be the study of the relations and interactions between men living in societies, including the conditions and the consequences of such interactions. Since social life is ' historical ', i.e. has duration in time, we must also study and disentangle the permanent from the changing elements in it, and seek to determine whether there are any regularities of sequence or general trends of change. Such a study clearly involves some form of morphology or the setting up of types of social life. This is implied in the mere division of social life into, say, ' economic ', ' religious ', ' moral ', ' legal ', etc. The further growth of the science necessitates finer classification, and the more consciously and deliberately we make the classification the better. Assuming such a refined morphology we must inquire further :

1. What elements in social life are functionally related, and the first step in this inquiry is to establish associations or correlations. This is the method employed by Tylor [2] and may be called the method of tracing adhesions. It will be recalled that he employed it in the study of the institutions connected with the family,

[1] Probleme der Wirtschaftsgeschichte, p. 191.
[2] *Journal of Anthrop. Inst.*, Vol. XVIII.

but it can be and has been generalized in anthropology and sociology. The use of the comparative method is here implied, since the adhesions are found in different societies.

2. We must ascertain whether there are any regularities in the changes of institutions, and whether the changes in any one institution are functionally correlated with changes in other institutions or other aspects of social life. Thus, for example, we may ask whether changes in the institutions of public justice are correlated with changes in the economic order. Now in dealing with peoples that have a history we can sometimes ascertain the changes which each has undergone and can show parallel changes in them directly. For example, in the study of the forms of capitalism in the countries of Europe, it has been shown that everywhere the industrial capitalism of the eighteenth century was preceded by a growth in commercial capitalism.[1] Similarly, we can trace large numbers of important parallel sequences in the languages or religions of the civilized peoples (cf. Otto [2]). On the other hand, in dealing with the primitive peoples, regularities of sequence cannot be established directly, since generally we know little about the changes which they have undergone and have to study them, so to speak, as at one moment of time. We can only establish sequences or orders of development by the method of tracing adhesions applied to an ideal typical series of changes. Thus, for example, we may find that a form of public justice 'high' in the series formulated for public justice is frequently associated with a form of economic growth 'high' in the series relating to the economic order. This is simply to employ the method of adhesions in tracing a serial order. Very often we can confirm conclusions reached

[1] Sée, H. : *Science et Philosophie de l'Histoire*, p. 163.
[2] *Religious Essays*.

by the aid of the comparative method in relation to the primitive peoples by direct historical evidence of parallel changes in a people whose historical development has been traced. This, I think, is the case, for example, with the institution of public justice. Compare, for example, Hobhouse's study of justice among the primitives with the history of English law by Pollock and Maitland.[1] It may be added that when a number of serial orders of change has been worked out for different aspects of social life and are shown or, more generally, assumed to be interrelated we obtain the notion of a 'general level' of a people's development and we speak of stages or phases of its civilization as a whole. Here there is always the danger of introducing ethical valuations. The 'higher' levels are taken to be 'better' or ideally more satisfactory. Personally I do not think the problem of ethical valuation is hopeless, but it need not necessarily be undertaken in a purely sociological inquiry. Some notion of a general level of development has been found practically necessary by all inquirers, since comparison is infinitely facilitated by looking for examples among peoples of more or less the same general level of civilization (cf. the remarks of Carveth Read [2]).

There are difficulties innumerable in the use of the method here outlined. The most important of these were noted in the discussion which followed Tylor's paper by Galton and others, and were, to some extent, met in his reply. Others are discussed in the *Simpler Peoples*, to which I may here refer.[3] I wish, however, to discuss certain ambiguities and difficulties of a more general nature, with the hope of clearing away important misconceptions.

[1] *History of English Law.*

[2] *Origin of Man and his Superstitions*, Preface.

[3] Hobhouse, Wheeler, and Ginsberg, *The Material Culture and Social Institutions of the Simpler Peoples.*

1. The establishment of associations between different aspects of social life or of correlations in sequences of change between them does not in itself enable us to establish what are called social laws or laws of social development. Association or correlation is not enough to yield causation. If we show a correlation between changes in the economic order and changes in the political order, we have not necessarily shown that they are causally related one to the other. The entities called economic and political are so ill-defined that we may not, in fact, be dealing with different events functionally interrelated but to a great extent with the same events looked at from different points of view. If this be once realized it will be seen that we cannot generalize any serial order of change found to hold good and extend it readily to other cases. The notion of unilinear sequences in social phenomena, everywhere repeated in the same sense or order, is really so naïve that it is difficult to take it seriously. It follows that the tracing of sequences in interrelation is not in itself sufficient to give us the 'direction' of social development (Müller-Lyer's *Richtungslinien* [1]). This will only be possible, if at all, when we have discovered the deeper causes of the sequences and can predict their continued operation under specified conditions.

2. The use of the method of 'adhesions' is rather to suggest hypotheses relating to causation or to check them. For example, the hypotheses put forward by Freud [2] to explain the laws of exogamy implies a necessary association between totemism and exogamy, and may be checked in part by inquiring whether the alleged association exists in fact, and whether the exceptions or deviations can be explained by reference to different conditions which are yet in harmony with the general theory. In giving this example, I am not suggesting

[1] *Die Phasen der Kultur.*

[2] *Totem and Tabu.*

that the only type of causal explanation in sociology is psychological in nature. Other factors are clearly involved. It is only when these factors have been isolated and universal propositions about them been established that it will be possible to speak of social laws.

I.—I conclude that the conception of stages of growth is still necessary and useful in sociology, and that it may be defended against the objections which have been raised against it.

II.—That its use does not commit us to any particular theory of social evolution, still less to any theory of progressive evolution; the tracing of sequences in orderly phases is a necessary preliminary to *any* theory of social development.

III.—What is now urgently needed is further work towards the establishment of a more complete social morphology and more refined analysis of the complex life of social institutions, with the object of facilitating the task of comparison, and ultimately, of causal explanation.

VI

EMOTION AND INSTINCT

MANY contributions have been made in recent psychological literature to the study of the nature of emotion, yet profound differences of opinion remain both as to the aetiology and function of emotional states. I propose in this paper to inquire whether a consistent theory can be put forward which would do justice to all the facts that recent investigations have brought to light. It would appear that the defects of most of the theories of emotion are due to the fact that they exaggerate some aspect or phase of emotion and claim for it exclusive or predominant value.

To begin with, several writers, among whom are some noted French psychologists, take what may be called the Stoic view that emotion is essentially a disturbance of the organism, a disease of the soul. In detail, such a view may take different forms. Thus, some writers regard emotion as instinct disrupted or broken up. For example, the emotion of fear is looked upon as a degenerate manifestation of the instinct of self-preservation, expressing itself in a useless and ill-adapted discharge of energy, the emotion of anger as an exaggerated form of the instincts of defence or aggression; emotion is thus *instinct raté*.[1] Others take the more general view that emotion is archaic instinct, and consists or results in the evocation of primitive, crude, and repressed instinctive responses; emotion is *instinct vieilli*.[2] The most

[1] cf. Larguier des Bancels, *Introd. à la Psychologie*, p. 328.
[2] Claparède, *Archives de Psychologie*, Vol. VII, p. 187.

far-reaching account on these lines is that given by Janet.[1] According to him, emotion arises when the individual finds himself suddenly in a situation presenting novel features, and requiring an extreme intensification of the normal impulses and tendencies. In such circumstances the subject is frequently so disturbed that his responses are inco-ordinate and diffuse, and there is insufficiency or inadequacy of action both of the lower and higher functions. The state so produced is emotion, and its essential characteristic is *insuffisance systématique de l'action.* Its producing causes are excessive suddenness, novelty or rapidity of events, prior depression or weakness of the subject or the emergence of repressed tendencies. In all such cases there is a fall of psychological tension, a diffuse discharge of energy, an evocation of lower and primitive impulses. No relief is found in this way, and there is therefore a tendency of the series of events just sketched, namely, excessive excitement, inadequate response, evocation of primitive impulses, to repeat itself indefinitely until there supervenes a new factor, namely, exhaustion. There is in fact a fundamental identity, according to Janet, between fatigue and emotion. Both result in a lowering of mental level, loss of the higher powers of adaptation, and an exaggeration of the more primitive tendencies. In the 'exciting emotions' inverse phenomena take place. Profound instincts come to the assistance of the failing impulses, the situation is dealt with adequately and successfully, and there is a general rise of mental level. It is to be noted that the psychologists who take the kind of view here briefly indicated generally protest against the finalism or teleology ascribed to emotional states, and emphasize the fact that emotion throws the organism into a state of chaos in which the subject makes few, if any, suitable adjustments to his environment. There

[1] cf. *Traité de Psychologie,* ed. Dumas, Vol. I, pp. 948–9.

is, they insist, an excessive and intense output of energy, which is not to be interpreted in terms of "*d'enfantines explications finalistes.*" [1]

In contrast with these and similar views, many writers, no doubt influenced by the work of Darwin, regard emotions as essentially adaptive reactions. Such writers generally insist on the connexion between instinct and emotion, but as to the precise nature of the connexion there is great difference of opinion. Thus Dr. McDougall regards the primary emotions as the affective aspects of the primary instincts. Instincts are then complex states containing within them emotions. On the other hand, Mr. Shand regards emotions as the wider systems containing or utilizing instincts for the realization of their ends. He denies that there is necessarily a specific connexion between given instincts and given emotions, and insists that emotions differ from instincts in being (*a*) more variable in their ends, (*b*) more variable in their means. Mr. Shand suggests, however, that in a sense the instincts are biologically prior. He says: 'We may perhaps assume that instincts have preceded definite emotions, that the excitement of the instinct was normally accompanied by an impulse that was felt with increasing intensity under conditions of arrest, and that when most intense bore some resemblance to an emotional state.' [2] This suggests a view now frequently held, though dismissed by McDougall as a 'curious dogma', that emotions arise when the instinctive tendencies are obstructed or in some way suspended. But on this point Mr. Shand's position is not quite clear to me, since he seems to regard emotions as more fundamental than instincts, while a complete development of the view hinted at in the above quotation would seem to imply that emotions were secondary.

[1] cf. Piéron, *Le Cerveau et la Pensée*, p. 310.
[2] *Foundations of Character*, p. 372.

On the question of the relation between instinct and emotion, mention must also be made of the views of some American psychologists. In the main they follow hints thrown out by William James.[1] Thus Woodworth[2] maintains that (i) emotion consists of internal responses, whilst instinct is outwardly directed ; (ii) that emotional response is of the nature of a preparatory reaction, while instinct is directed towards the end reaction. Emotions, in other words, are states of preparedness for instinctive action. In the main this is also the view of Prof. Watson : 'When the adjustments called out by the stimulus are internal and confined to the subject's body, we have emotion, for example, blushing ; when the stimulus leads to the adjustments of the body as a whole to objects, we have instinct, for example, defence responses.'[3]

Reference must also be made to some results of recent physiological work on the emotions, in so far as they bear upon the problem of the nature of emotion. They may be summed up as follows :

1. Emotional reactions are very diffusive in nature, frequently involving an overflow and discharge of energy, resulting in responses which cannot be shown, apart from preconceived theories, to be necessarily adaptive.

2. The somatic and visceral concomitants or constituents of emotion are of the nature partly of preparatory readjustments, partly expressive of the diffuse excitement set up, partly also perhaps of a conflict of tendencies. Cannon stresses the utility of the visceral changes in fear and rage as preparing the organism for the violent action that is to follow. But he has been criticized on the ground (i) that he has ignored the 'asthenic' or depressed phases of emotion, (ii) that he

[1] Cf. *Principles*, Vol. II, p. 442. [2] *Psychology*, p. 134.
[3] Ibid., p. 216.

has exaggerated the adaptiveness of the visceral changes, and (iii) that he assumes somewhat too readily that the visceral changes are similar or identical in different emotional states.[1] It will be readily seen that by judicious selection support can be found in physiological work for both the contrasted views of emotion set out above. A satisfactory theory of emotion, it seems to me, should do justice to at least the following points:

1. It should account for the fact that psychologists have been able to regard emotion as on the one hand pathological aberrations or disturbances, and on the other hand as organizing or systematizing agencies in the development of character.

2. It should offer an explanation of the relation between instinct and emotion which would take into consideration (*a*) the diffusive character of the emotional responses, and the, at any rate partial, similarity of organic disturbance in different emotional states; (*b*) the plasticity and variability of the adjustments evoked in or by emotional states.

The first requirement can be met by means of a distinction, familiar enough to common sense, and recently emphasized in the work of Dumas, between emotion in the stage of the first shock, and emotion as it is experienced when the subject has recovered somewhat and is preparing for suitable action. In the first phase there are few if any suitable adjustments. On the contrary, the reactions are diffuse, there is an excessive liberation and overflow of energy, or else in the depressing emotions, conflicting tendencies are set up, resulting in inhibitions and lowering of mental level generally. Apart from really pathological cases, however, the organism reasserts itself, a selection takes place from among the impulses incited, and this is accompanied by organic changes which partly express

[1] cf. Dumas, *Traité*, pp. 625–9.

the operation of the conflicting tendencies, but partly also are of the nature of preparatory readjustments whose function is to attune the body for the requisite action which is to supervene. It is at this stage that emotions can be spoken of as states possessed of definite recognizable characters, conative, affective, and cognitive. At this stage, moreover, the emotion is no longer diffuse, though it remains plastic, capable of selecting and utilizing varying responses to meet the requirements of the situation. The function of the emotion is now to organize, to lead to adaptive and persistent behaviour. The distinction between the emotion-shock and the emotion-state is not, of course, an absolute distinction ; the shock may be slight and of short duration, while in other cases it may be very profound, and the subject may not emerge from the diffuse excitement set up. There are also intermediate forms in which the two phases are intermingled in an intricate manner and cases when the instinctive or habit responses selected prove inadequate and the subject relapses into the shock phase. Generally, nevertheless, the two phases can be distinguished, and the recognition of this distinction enables us to do justice at once to what has been called the Stoic view of emotion, according to which it is pathological in character, and the views of those who regard emotion as essentially adaptive. Both these views are partial and over-emphasize certain aspects of the emotional experience at the expense of the rest. Emotions are not necessarily pathological, but they become so either (*a*) when they never emerge from the stage of diffused and excessive discharge of energy and conflict of impulses characteristic of the emotion-shock, or (*b*) when the selection of impulses is inappropriate and results not in a due balance of the conflicting tendencies, but in an over-emphasis of some and an undue repression of others. On the other hand, all emotions contain features indicative of general and diffuse disturbance, and their adaptive character, frequently exemplified clearly enough in the later phases, must not be taken for granted but studied in detail in each case.

We may now approach the question of the relation between instinct and emotion. There appear to be at least three divergent views of the nature of this relation. They may be briefly indicated as follows:

1. Emotion is the affective aspect of instinct.

2. Emotion is a wider system utilizing instinct but having wider and more variable ends and means than instinct.

3. The affective side of instinct is not as such emotional, but becomes so under conditions of obstruction or excess of excitement.

One difficulty of dealing satisfactorily with this problem is that there is no more agreement regarding the nature of instinct than there is regarding that of emotion, and this lack of agreement, though occasionally due to verbal ambiguity, does often rest upon real differences of substance. Another difficulty arises from the fact that in the discussions of this problem several rather different issues are involved which have not been sufficiently discriminated. They may perhaps be set out thus:

(*a*) Do emotions always arise in connexion with instincts?

(*b*) Have emotions ends distinct from those of instinct, or are emotions preparatory states for the realization of ends determined by instinct?

(*c*) If or when emotions do arise in connexion with instincts, is there any specific relation between them, such that certain emotions are especially characteristic of, or peculiar to, certain instincts?

These questions cannot here be answered in detail,

but our general attitude to them may be briefly indicated. As to (*a*) and (*b*), which are closely connected, it should be noted, firstly, that emotions occasionally *arise* not as the result of failure or over-excitement of instinct, but rather because the subject finds himself in a situation for which there is no instinctive response readily available, as when a child experiences fear when he is suddenly dropped from the hands. Secondly, whether emotions are always dependent on instinct depends on the view we take as to the ultimate ends of action. If we regard the latter as ultimately prescribed by instinct, then directly or indirectly the emotions must be related to instincts; if, on the other hand, we take the view that some ends of action are not instinctively determined, there can be no necessary connexion in all cases between emotion and instinct. The view here taken is that in all cases ends are determined by what may be called impulse-feeling, but the latter may be incited by interests which are connected with instincts, by innate interests other than instinctive, by acquired interests due to sentiments built up in the course of the individual's experience. Emotion is heightened impulse-feeling which may arise in connexion with any or all these interests. If the impulses and feelings involved, when the emotion is evoked and in course of the operation of the emotion are instinctive, then the emotion may be said to be secondary on instinct; if, on the other hand, the interests involved have been remoulded by experience, the emotion is clearly equally mixed.

As to (*c*), Mr. Shand has clearly shown [1] that (i) an instinct may be excited without necessarily involving an innately determined specific emotion, (ii) the same primary emotion may be connected with a plurality of instincts, (iii) the same instinct may subserve different

[1] *Foundations of Character.*

emotions. Dr. McDougall himself recognizes that the connexion cannot be equally close in all cases. It should be remembered that in the shock phase of emotion conflicting tendencies are frequently set going, and that later a selection takes place, which is, we have seen, plastic and variable.

It is in fact in the notion of plasticity that the key to the nature of emotion is to be found. In order to make this clear, we must consider the nature of instinct. By instinct I understand a series of reflex or sensori-motor acts held together by an underlying mood or feeling of tension, which persists until the end of the series is attained. Instinct is not a mere concatenation of reflexes. There must be in instinct a continued interest, sustaining, directing and grading the inherited typical reactions. There must be something, in fact, which accounts for the persistence with varied effort characteristic of such behaviour as is exemplified, for example, in instinctive hunting. The function of the feeling of interest, which may be characterized negatively as one of tension, and positively as one of worth-whileness, is to prompt and sustain action until the tension is relieved, in other words, to make possible persistence with varied effort. The function of emotion, it is now suggested, is to reinforce such persistence, while increasing the plasticity of the behaviour requisite for dealing with the situation. In any given instinct the amount of the variability of the component acts is limited to the typical reactions characteristic of the instinct. Emotion is capable, as Mr. Shand has amply shown, of varying the means necessary for the attainment of its ends and of calling to its aid different sets of acts as occasion requires. It is not true to say either that emotion is the affective element of instinct, or even that emotion is the affective element of instinct heightened under conditions of over-excitement or obstruction. The relation between the two is not so simple. The emotional reaction begins, no doubt, generally with heightened impulse feeling of instincts, but in the shock phase it is extremely diffuse, and later, when it ceases to be diffuse, it remains plastic and capable of utilizing not merely the instincts which gave rise to it but other responses, instinctive and non-instinctive as well, though uniting them all by means of a persistent feeling tone, which gives definite character to the emotion as a complex whole.

If this view is correct, we should expect emotions to arise in conditions in which persistent behaviour is necessary but not satisfied by immediate instinct. This is in fact what we find, for emotions occur :

1. When normal responses fail, as when an infant experiences fear as the result of the sudden removal of means of support.

2. When instinctive action is delayed or obstructed, as in the many forms of anger or disgust, or as in the emotion of suspense.

3. When prolonged action is necessary for the satisfaction of instinctive impulses, as in the joyous emotions.

4. When the object or situation which usually calls forth instinctive or other impulses is temporarily or irretrievably removed, as in the varieties of sorrow or grief.

5. When reactions are roused with a suddenness for which the subject is not prepared.

Emotions then appear to be states of tension or maladjustment, arising from conditions of conflict or delay, or failure of normal response or suddenness of excitement or over-stimulation, passing over into more or less adaptive states, exhibiting prolonged and persistent behaviour of a varied and plastic character. They are essentially secondary, or, as Prof. Stout says, parasitic in character, depending upon prior impulse-feeling or interests, or arising when normal reactions fail.

Let us check this view by a brief reference to a number of emotions. Fear arises generally when normal responses are not immediately available, as in the case of the infant observed by Watson and mentioned above, which showed fear when suddenly dropped from the hands ; or else when the instinctive reactions evoked by a situation of danger, e.g., flight, are obstructed or fail. It has been plausibly argued that normal or unimpeded flight is not accompanied by the emotion of fear. On the view here suggested, the function of fear, when the latter gets beyond the diffuse shock state, is to lend persistence to the endeavours of the organism to free itself from danger by utilizing various instinctive responses, such as flight, immobility, shamming dead, or even fighting, as occasion requires. Fear is thus not the affective aspect of the instinct of flight, but rather a diffuse disturbance of the organism evoking various impulses and persisting until relief is found, and having a characteristic feeling tone which accompanies the impulses and organic changes involved in the total processes set up. Dr. McDougall shows that terror is due to the conflict of incompatible impulses. Some amount of conflict, it seems to me, is involved even in milder cases of fear, that is, incipient movements are checked and varied until one or other of the impulses evoked gains dominance.

The case of anger affords clear support to the theory above suggested. Anger is clearly a disturbance depending upon the prior operation of other impulses. Thus 'destructive' anger arises when the demands of some powerful impulse, for example, hunger or sex, cannot be met, or more generally in cases of obstruction which reach a certain intensity. Anger, which aims not at destruction necessarily, but at the overcoming of opposition, obviously presupposes interference with existing impulse. What Mr. Shand calls retrospective anger or revenge arises from baffled impulse seeking relief. So again the anger which expresses itself in threats implies a delayed or checked response of the impulse to attack. The adaptive character of anger must not be exaggerated, for very often it leads to such disturbances as to make appropriate action difficult, but in its more organized forms, it is generally agreed, it tends to invigorate and reinforce appropriate impulses and to call forth reserves of energy not otherwise available.

The emotion of disgust seems to arise in pronounced form in situations which call forth the instincts of ejection, spitting out, shaking, pushing away, and when conditions are present which delay or prolong these responses. In the absence of such conditions the feeling tone of the instincts does not reach emotional intensity. Of repugnance, Mr. Shand has distinguished five varieties, namely, that which springs from the sensations of taste and smell, from vision, from colours and noises, from certain experiences of conflict, as when one is kept in a situation in spite of one's desire or impulse to change it. I suggest that in all these cases emotional intensity is only reached when the object or situation calling forth the various avoiding reactions persists and cannot be promptly dealt with. A certain amount of obstruction or conflict seems to be required for the feeling of repugnance to become truly emotional.

The emotion of wonder is secondary, and presupposes baffled curiosity. When the exploratory movements or manipulation characteristic of curiosity can be carried out readily there is no emotion. It is only when there is a check to action and an uncertainty of appropriate behaviour that wonder arises, and its function is clearly to keep the object of curiosity before the mind and to lend persistence to the endeavour to ascertain its nature.

The various forms of sorrow arise from the frustration of primary impulse, desire, or sentiment. Sorrow is essentially a state of maladjustment due to the loss, temporary or enduring, of an object to which powerful impulses had come to be attached, in which the impulses persist, though they can no longer find expression in the accustomed manner. As in all the emotions, so in the various forms of sorrow, a sort of selection takes place from among the reverberating impulses set up with the first shock. In the milder varieties, which are caused by the loss of an object or change in an affective situation, not beyond all remedy or hope of recovery, sorrow seems to have the function of making the subject cling tenderly to the object of the attachment, to keep it before the mind, to call up associations connected with it, in a manner which partially satisfies the impulses originally relating to the object, while at the same time the absence in reality of that object stimulates the endeavour for its recovery. In the severer forms of sorrow the loss is felt as irremediable, the disorganization set up is more extensive and profound, the various impulses which originally found satisfaction in the object seek expression in vain. In some cases this may lead to mental depression and inertia, in others to the emotion of resignation, which in a sense is an adaptive reaction. For in the very act of resigning oneself one asserts oneself ; one has, so to say, found a method of dealing with the demands of impulses once imperious and is able to let them appear in consciousness, while depriving them of the power of compelling action which they once possessed. In other cases, again, sorrow is active, expressing itself in violent protest or lamentation, though even in such cases there seems to be present an element of resignation. From the mixture in various proportions of resignation and revolt there emerge the various forms of grief, culminating in despair. In all forms there is involved a conflict of tendencies, and the degree of adaptiveness or utility to the organism of the emotion depends upon the extent to which the subject succeeds in selecting from, and finding ways of satisfying, the impulses incited, by a reorganization of the affective life, by finding new outlets for the impulses, or by finding new interests compensating for the loss sustained. The distinction sometimes drawn between active and passive sorrow is one of degree only. No sorrow seems completely passive. It always involves frustrated impulse seeking satisfaction. On the other hand, the most violent sorrow seems to have an element of tender resignation.

In the joyous emotions the fundamental function of emotion as an organizing agency, namely, that of prompting and sustaining persistent effort, is readily to be traced. For joy generally arises when unimpeded adaptation to a situation, or exercise of faculty, is possible and easy but not automatic. This may happen either when a new object is suddenly secured which releases a variety of impulses, or when impulses hitherto held in check are suddenly liberated. In both cases there is a general diffuse excitement, a feeling of released energy which gradually gains in definiteness, and, by selection or relevant impulses, maintains the object of the emotion before the mind and secures adaptive behaviour towards it. Joy seems to involve the prior existence in relation to its object of more than one impulse, or at least in the case of one impulse the possibility of progressive and sustained satisfaction. For the immediate satisfaction of a single impulse, however intense and sudden, hardly conduces to joy but merely to pleasure. The function of the emotion of joy seems to be to prolong the exercise of the relevant impulses by maintaining the object upon which they are directed, and the relation of the self to that object in a state which will make sustained and progressive satisfaction possible. This is true not only of the active joys but also of the serene joys. For serenity involves a certain variability and play of impulses, and does not result from the monotonous satisfaction of a single impulse. A certain amount of diffusiveness, followed by persistent though plastic behaviour, which we have seen to be characteristic of emotion, is thus clearly to be discerned in the emotion of joy.

A curious case is the emotion of loneliness. Dr. McDougall [1] regards it as the affective aspect of the gregarious instinct. It is clear that this is only plausible, if by the gregarious instinct is meant, not the tendency to be or remain with the herd, but rather to seek it. For loneliness is only felt when away from the herd, and cannot consequently be the emotion accompanying the experience of being with the herd. In any event, the emotion of loneliness is too complex to be accounted for in terms of the affective aspect of the herd instinct. It seems to be a diffuse emotion, resulting from the obstruction or failure of a variety of impulses stimulated by the presence of one's fellows, the absence of that give and take, responding and evoking response, characteristic of social life.

Brief reference may also be made to tender emotion. Mr. Shand has shown [2] that this is a complex and derived emotion, involving a subtle intermingling of joy and sorrow. It thus rests upon a balance of conflicting tendencies and implies a persistent and lingering mood.

It would seem, then, from a survey of the emotions discussed above, that the formulae which have hitherto been suggested to express the relation between instinct and emotion are inadequate. Thus to say that emotion is the affective aspect of instinct may be plausible in the case of fear and anger, but is not helpful when applied to joy and sorrow, suspense, disappointment,

[1] *Outline of Psychology*, p. 324.

[2] In Stout's *Groundwork of Psychology*, Chap. XVI.

and many other emotions. To meet these cases Dr. McDougall has been led to add to the list of his primary emotions a number of 'derived emotions' which he defines as 'emotion which is not constantly correlated with any one impulse or tendency, but rather may arise in the course of the operation of any strong impulse or tendency'. If our account is true, all emotion is derived emotion in the sense here laid down. For, as we have seen, emotions arise when impulses are obstructed or delayed or in the presence of incompatible impulses, or when the organism finds itself in a situation for which it has no ready response, or else when the impulses incited by a situation require prolonged and varied action for their satisfaction.

Nor is it an adequate account of emotion to say that emotion is the affective aspect of instinct heightened in conditions of strain or obstruction or over-excitement. For though emotions may and do begin in this way, their character is by no means due entirely to the feeling tone of the impulses or instincts in which they had their origin. Emotions, as we have seen, are very diffuse disturbances, and when they come to have qualitative definiteness, the latter is due to an assemblage of factors going far beyond the impulses which were the starting-point of the emotion.

Our view is perhaps nearest to that of Mr. Shand, but the latter seems to suffer from (*a*) an exaggeration of the adaptive character of emotions and a failure to emphasize sufficiently the diffusiveness of some of the phases through which emotions pass; (*b*) from not making sufficiently clear that impulse is the primary thing, and that emotions are in a sense secondary, or, as Prof. Stout says, 'parasitic', or, to put this in another way, that the ends of emotions are ultimately traceable to fundamental instincts or other impulses. But Mr. Shand has the great merit of having pointed out the plasticity of emotions, and of having worked out a theory of the sentiments according to which their value largely lies, among other things, in the fact that they further increase the range of reactions towards a given object, and thus prevent emotions from becoming morbid.[1] It is here suggested that this notion of plasticity can be carried back to the interpretation of the instincts, and that the key to the movement from instinct to sentiment is to be found in the need for persistence with plastic and varied effort.

[NOTE.—Since writing this article, I have had the advantage of reading the typescript of Mr. Shand's paper on 'Character'. I find that, as now stated by him, his views are not open to the criticisms I have ventured to raise against them.]

[1] cf. especially Mr. Shand's article on 'The Relation between Complex and Sentiment' (*British Journal of Psychology*, Vol. XIII).

VII

THE PLACE OF INSTINCT IN SOCIAL THEORY [1]

IT is fitting that I should begin this inaugural address by expressing my sense of the great honour which the University of London has conferred upon me in appointing me to succeed the late Prof. Hobhouse. Very few workers either in England or abroad have done as much as Hobhouse towards the promotion of the scientific study of sociology, or made significant contributions to so many of its fields of inquiry. No one, I will venture to say, had such a profound grasp of the relations in which the various social sciences stand to each other and to philosophy, or held the balance between them so finely. To follow such a master is indeed a heavy task, and I should approach it with but little confidence were it not for the knowledge that Hobhouse himself often expressed his eager desire that I should be his successor, which encourages me in the hope that if I cannot rival his achievements, I may yet make some contribution to the development of the science of which he laid the foundations.

There are two points in Hobhouse's attitude to science and philosophy that I should like to stress as particularly relevant just now. Hobhouse, like every one else, was deeply impressed with the revolutionary changes that have recently been occurring in the physical sciences, and he felt that these changes must have their repercussions on the social and mental sciences. But

[1] An inaugural lecture delivered at the London School of Economics on December 2nd 1930.

he had no sympathy at all with those who find in these developments arguments for subjectivism and vague mysticism. Their importance lay rather in the liberating influence they were likely to exert on the general mind in encouraging the more independent study of aspects of reality other than the physical. This liberating influence was due, according to him, to two things; firstly, the newer views destroyed the belief in materialism proper—that is, the belief that matter was the only real and self-subsistent entity or substance, and tended to replace it by the view that what was called matter was rather a way of describing certain modes of behaviour or process. Secondly, on the side of the theory of knowledge, the recent changes tended to show that striking successes in measurement might be achieved on the basis of hypotheses which were eventually discarded, and that in questions of underlying theory physical science was capable of changes of front quite comparable with those for which philosophy has often been derided. In short, the rigidity and primacy of the physical sciences has been shaken, and though this is no justification for the mystery-mongering in which many people seem to be indulging now, it does justify us in putting forward a demand for autonomy on behalf of the sciences dealing with mind, with conduct, and with art. It seems to me that this demand for autonomy ought to be made especially for psychology and sociology, which seem at present specially exposed to the influence of mechanical conceptions. The formula of the stimulus response so widely used by the Behaviourists, the effort to account for mental integration in terms of a linking up of reflexes and their conditioning, and some forms of the instinct theory which lend countenance to the view that man is a bundle of inborn tendencies, all show the hold that a mechanistic neurology has upon psychology. I do not wish to dogmatize about the value of neurological studies, but merely to insist on the importance of a direct experimental study of behaviour without committing ourselves in advance to the assumption that all processes must necessarily be capable of interpretation in terms borrowed from the physical sciences. I should like to quote in this connexion a statement recently made by a distinguished neurologist:

'The development of psychology up to the present has been strongly influenced by neurological theory. The frantic search for sources of motivation and of emotion in visceral activity, though initiated by introspective analysis, has been supported by the faith that the nervous system is only a conductor, having no sources of energy within itself. Our preoccupation with analysis of learning by trial and error, the denial of association by similarity, the belief that the transfer of training can only occur through the training of common synapses—these are the result of the belief that learning is simply a linking together of elementary reflexes. The doctrine that the intelligent solution of problems results only through random activity and selection and that intelligence is an algebraic sum of multitudinous capacities is largely a deduction from the reflex theory . . . they may or may not be true, but their truth must be demonstrated by experiment and cannot be assumed on a background of questionable neurology.'[1]

In view of the fact that the extreme forms of Behaviourism have already revealed their sterility and inadequacy in psychology, it would, so it seems to me, be a great pity if they were allowed, as they show signs of doing, to invade the field of social studies.

The need for independence or autonomy in sociology is especially obvious in relation to biology. There is undoubtedly a whole range of inquiries in which biology may have much to contribute towards a scientific

[1] Professor Lashley, *Psychological Review*, January 1930.

sociology.[1] But it is of the greatest importance that in such studies our conclusions should be based on a direct examination of the facts and not on vague analogies derived from animal biology, or on biological principles not directly verified from human experience. A good many studies of what is called racial decay or degeneration consist almost entirely of speculations and deductions having very little support in historical fact. To take one example. The decay of Rome is often interpreted biologically in terms of what is called the dying out of the best. But according to recent work in ancient history it is becoming extremely doubtful whether there took place anything that could be described as racial decay in any sense. A great authority like Rostovtseff tells us that historians do not now recognize that there was even a decay of civilization in these periods, but rather a shifting of values; and it is becoming increasingly clear that the explanation of these cultural changes will have to be sought in cultural terms.[2] In general, in biological discussions of race deterioration much too much seems to me to be based on deductions of what must happen in accordance with the principle of natural selection, without any proof being adduced either that natural selection is an important agent in human progress or that deterioration is in fact occurring as a result of human effort to control natural selection.

The other point on which I should like to lay stress is also one upon which Hobhouse insisted. The social sciences are tending to break up into a large number of specialisms. There is even greater need now than there was in the time of Comte for a science which should give a *vue d'ensemble* of social life and which should bring together the result of the manifold specialisms and show

[1] cf. Chap. I, p. 17.
[2] cf. 'The Decay of the Ancient World and its Economic Explanations' (*The Economic History Review*, January 1930).

their bearing upon the interpretation of society regarded as a whole. It is perhaps arrogant for any sociologist to claim that he can know enough of the social sciences and of other sciences to which he must necessarily appeal, to be able to utilize them effectively for the purpose of his synthesis. I am ready to admit also that what has so far been achieved towards such synthesis is slight in comparison with what remains to be done. Yet the effort must be made. It is a necessary part of such an effort to examine critically from time to time the use that is made in sociology of categories and principles of explanation derived from other sciences. I have chosen for my subject the conception of Instinct which is of interest because of the very wide use which has been made of it by sociologists and because of the fierce criticism that has been of late directed against it.

The sociologist who goes to psychology for an account of instinct finds a most anomalous state of affairs. On the one hand we find such an authority as McDougall claiming that the instincts constitute the sole source of human motivation, and Dr. Ernest Jones declaring that the study of the instincts is in many respects yet the most fundamental in all psychology. Prof. Alexander appears to have sufficient faith in the value of the notion of instinct to base on it his theory of morality, art, and science. Thus, according to him, truth has value because it satisfies the instinct of curiosity; art satisfies the instinct of constructiveness; morality is the art which satisfies the instinct of gregariousness.[1] On the other hand, Prof. Laird dismisses the appeal to instincts as based on a pseudo science which is yet in the metaphysical stage of occult qualities or at best mistakes the names of classes for authentic causes in nature.[2] In America the battle about instincts has raged fast and

[1] *Journal of Philosophical Studies*, April 1928.
[2] *Idea of Value*, p. 40.

furious, and in many authoritative works the notion is discredited, though very few people really abandon it in the end, and there are signs that the attack has exhausted itself. It is interesting to inquire into the sources of this campaign. In part it was undoubtedly a healthy reaction against the abuses of the notion of instinct in sociological literature. Prof. Bernard tells us that he discovered approximately six thousand separate classes of more or less complex instincts as distinguished from reflexes under nearly fifteen thousand different forms.[1] Some of the examples he cites from competent authorities show the readiness with which mere naming is substituted for explanation and analysis. In the main, however, the scepticism in regard to instinct has a different origin. In the first place, the campaign is part of what may be called the flight from the mind characteristic of the Behaviourist movement. The use of such notions as impulse, effort, end, or purpose, is anathema to Behaviourists. Secondly, the movement expresses a wish to believe in the possibility of moulding human nature indefinitely by changes produced in the environment. 'To-morrow,' says Prof. Bernard, 'belongs to the student of environment just as the past fifty years belonged to the student of inheritance.' While sympathizing with the arguments which lay stress on the importance of environmental agencies in the development of the mental life, I feel certain that in the form which they assume in Behaviouristic writings they are doomed to disappointment. There are inborn differences between individuals which set a limit to their educability; and though we cannot measure with any precision the relative potency of environmental and hereditary factors, we can be fairly sure that there is no ground for returning to the view which regards mind as a *tabula rasa*, or to the extreme environmentalism of the eighteenth century.

[1] *Monist*, April 1927.

It is, I think, an irony of fate that people so powerfully inspired by a wish to believe should be engaged so fiercely in trying to prove that there are no wishes at all.

I wish now to make an attempt towards a definition and clarification of the concept of instinct, and then to discuss its applicability in sociology. The best approach is still to be found in the description given by Darwin. He says: 'An action which we ourselves require experience to enable us to perform when performed by an animal, more especially by a young one, without experience, and when performed by many individuals in the same way without their knowing for what purpose it is performed, is usually said to be instinctive, but I could show that none of these characters are universal. A little dose of judgment or reason often comes into play even with animals low in the scale of nature.'[1] Amplifying these remarks we may say that the term Instinct covers those forms of behaviour consisting of a series of interrelated acts which (1) are directed towards an end or goal, (2) exhibit a certain adaptability and persistence with varied effort which might connote intelligence, but which (3) are performed in circumstances in which, in the absence of experience and taking into consideration the level of mentality otherwise attained by the organism in question, there can be no knowledge of the end nor deliberate and conscious contrivance on the part of the individual. The activities involved, for example, in the nest-building of birds, are complex, varied, and adapted to their surroundings. Yet we cannot attribute to a bird at its first performance a knowledge of the end in the sense of the completed nest, and we can only describe its behaviour by assuming an impulse towards an unknown goal innately determined which persists until the end is achieved. The impulse must not be conceived as a force or animistic spirit acting 'upon' the organism; it is

[1] *Origin*, p. 320.

simply what the animal feels while the instinct is operative, and which lends persistence, unity, and continuity to the series of efforts involved. Further, the instinct is not a mere pattern of behaviour or 'motor mechanism'. We must assume a persistent conation regulating and sustaining a course of action and rendering it adaptive and variable within limits.

To make this notion of instinct clear, it is necessary to compare it with reflex action, habit, intelligence, and emotion. This is a task more appropriate for a book than for a short paper, and I hope I shall be excused if my treatment appears summary and dogmatic. The identification of instinct with reflex activity was taught by Herbert Spencer, and his view has been revived by the Behaviourists and the followers of Pavlov. We may grant that some of the criteria which are alleged as differentiating reflexes from instincts are inadequate. Pavlov shows [1] that neither complexity nor length of the train of actions, nor dependence upon the total internal state of the organism, is peculiar to instincts but may be illustrated from actions which are admittedly reflex. But his arguments do not appear to touch the really important points at issue. In the first place, recent work has tended to bring out clearly the variability of the component parts of instinctive activities relatively to the end pursued. Instincts do not possess the stereotyped character which we should expect if they were nothing but reflexes. Reference may be made here to the work of the Peckhams on wasps, of Wasmann on ants, of Baltzer on spiders, and, in America, to the works of Tolman, Craig, Hamilton, and others. In so far as reflexes enter at all into instinctive acts, they admit of varied combinations in a series which as a whole nevertheless exhibits unmistakable unity and continuity. There is persistence with varied effort, and obstacles are

[1] *Conditioned Reflexes*, pp. 9–11.

set aside by methods which vary from case to case until the end is attained. The notion that to each observable variation in the responses there corresponds a precise variation in the stimulus would require us to assume mechanisms of infinite complexity in the lower organisms credible only to those who are dominated by mechanistic dogmas. It may be noted further that in contrast with reflex acts, instinctive behaviour is active—' the bird seeks the material for its nest, the predatory animal stalks its game '. In short, instinctive action does not present the appearance of a summation of reflexes, and it has unity and continuity amidst variation of its component parts which points to the hypothesis that the animal is acting with some sense, however dim, of forward direction or prospective reference. It may be noted that even the most ardent upholders of the reflex theory cannot proceed very far without using words having teleological reference. Thus Pavlov speaks of an investigatory reflex, or the ' what is it ' reflex set going by a change in the situation. He even goes farther than most psychologists in inventing what he calls ' the freedom reflex ' in order to explain the curious behaviour of a dog which would not remain quiet when it was constrained in the stand. We may well ask just what is the stimulus in these cases in terms of the sensory fibres excited ?

In the second place, a still more radical objection to the reflex theory of instinct is that it affords a poor basis for a theory of mental growth and development. Here, of course, use is made of the notion of conditioning. ' It is obvious,' says Pavlov, ' that the different kinds of habit based on training, education, and discipline of any sort are nothing but a long chain of conditioned reflexes.' And this, in spite of the fact that only a few lines above on the same page he had said himself that ' it would be the height of presumption to regard these first steps in elucidating the physiology of the cortex as solving the intricate problems of the higher activities in man when, in fact, at the present stage of our work no detailed application of its results to man is yet permissible.' [1] So far from the doctrine of the conditioned reflex affording an adequate basis for dealing with human behaviour, it is extremely doubtful whether it throws much light on the phenomena of learning in the animal world. I may here refer to an extremely instructive article by Lashley in *The Foundations of Experimental Psychology* which seems to me to show conclusively that the facts of training experiments are not in harmony with the theory of the specificity of conduction paths implied in the reflex theory since, on the one hand, responses can be shown to be independent of the particular sensory cells stimulated, and, on the other, habits acquired do not necessarily utilize patterns identical with those employed during the process of learning. In another place Lashley goes so far as to assert that ' in the study of cerebral functions we seem to have reached a point when the reflex theory is no longer profitable either for a formulation of problems or for an understanding of the phenomena of integration '. [2] It may be added that Sherrington has pointed out that in Pavlov's experiments the ground act—that is, the unconditioned response—was not a pure reflex but may have included large psychical reactions as well. He says: ' Secretion of saliva in response to food in the mouth has been used as a ground act, and in terming it an unconditioned reflex we must remember that although secretion of saliva can, after severe curtailment of the nervous system, be obtained as a pure reflex, it yet, as obtained in the feeding responses of the intact animal, is but one component of an immense reaction with emotional and other mental accompaniments involving wide regions of the pallium.' [1]

[1] p. 395. [2] *Psychological Review*, January 1930.

As far as I can see, the comparative study of the processes of learning in the animal world reveals the complete inadequacy of the theory of the conditioned reflex as a principle of explanation, and justifies us on the contrary in ascribing conational elements to the lowest forms of life.

In one form the theory that instincts are really habits is old. Both Darwin and Romanes distinguish between primary instincts explained by natural selection, and secondary instincts which were inherited habits. Wundt also thought that instincts were movements originally voluntary but wholly or partly mechanized in the course of genetic evolution. In this form the theory involves the transmission of acquired characters for which, it appears, there is no independent convincing evidence. It has, however, appeared in a new form in recent American psychological literature. According to this view, instincts are really reflexes organized into habit patterns as a result of experience in contact with the environment. In so far as this is intended to refer to the behaviour of adult human beings, there is obviously an element of truth in it. No one would maintain that in normal adult behaviour we get cases of pure instinct. In any concrete behaviour there are at most only instinctive components overlaid by acquired and partly mechanized forms of action. But as a theory of the nature of instinct it misses the essential point. In the lower animals at any rate we often find orderly sequences of behaviour which cannot be explained either as acquired by conditioning or as the result of habits fixed by trial and error, for they often appear practically perfect promptly after birth where there can have been no prior experience. Moreover, if the view of instinct which I have been suggesting above is correct, instinct contains as an essential core an element of impulse-feeling or

[1] *Encyclopaedia Britannica*, 14th Ed., Vol. IV, p. 6.

conation, and thus differs from habit, which operates automatically or mechanically. The element of variability which differentiates instincts from reflexes clearly marks them out also from fixed habits. It may be added that on the basis of habit without the element of impulse no account can be given of learning, since the essence of habit is conservation of old reactions, and what we need in dealing with learning is a factor that will account for selective variation.

The relation between instinct and intelligence is still much disputed. Most of the discussions appear to suffer from the extraordinary cloudiness of the notion of intelligence which the numerous symposia that have been held on the subject have not succeeded in clearing up. There are several not very illuminating biologically flavoured definitions of intelligence. Thus we are told that intelligence is the power to adapt oneself to novel situations, the faculty with which old responses can be brought to bear on new situations, or, again, general mental adaptability to new problems and conditions of life, and the like. These definitions may indicate more or less correctly the occasions on which intelligence comes into play, but they throw no light on the mental processes at all. Other definitions take refuge in verbal substitutes such as thinking, knowledge, etc. Many of the mental testers give up the job of defining entirely and take intelligence to consist in whatever powers the mental tests test. There are, however, two recent attempts at defining intelligence, namely, those made by Prof. Spearman and Prof. Wolf, to which I should like specially to refer. Prof. Spearman reduces cognitive experience to three forms, namely, immediate experience or enjoyment, by which he appears to mean the power of knowing one's own experience, the eduction of relations, and the eduction of correlates. In addition to these, which are taken to constitute a unitary factor 'g', there are also special factors 's' peculiar to specific operations. Prof. Spearman says very little about instinct. In his earlier work he suggests that instincts cannot possess any separate cognitive form, since the three processes enumerated cover all the forms of cognitive experience. In *The Abilities of Man* he repudiates what he describes as the biology of the penny-in-the-slot description, which accounts for behaviour in terms of specific instincts touched off by specific stimuli (though strangely enough he seems ready to accept an instinct in girls to play with mechanical toys). Prof. Wolf narrows the scope of intelligence to the apprehension of certain types of relations, namely, causal or logical relations, which he designates 'connexions'. Simple relations of space and time, likeness and difference, are apprehended in direct perception; connexions, on the other hand, require a certain amount of unravelling and a degree of inference. Intelligence as the apprehension of connexions is dependent upon other cognitive functions, e.g. memory, imagination, sensibility, but is distinguishable from them. It varies enormously in the degree of clarity with which connexions are apprehended and the range or sphere of objects within which it operates successfully. Neither Prof. Spearman's nor Prof. Wolf's views have as yet been applied to comparative psychology. I am not clear whether Prof. Spearman's theory is intended to apply outside the human sphere. I doubt whether at any rate the eduction of correlates can be proved for the higher animals. Prof. Wolf's definition would appear to be more manageable, since clarity, articulateness and range afford useful differentiae in the classification of types of behaviour. In applying these views of intelligence to the problem before us, it would seem that persistence with varied effort is not in itself a test of intelligence, nor is that form of learning by experience which consists in the acquisition of co-ordinated modes of behaviour by habit or crude trial and error. In its relation to impulse, the function of intelligence seems to consist (1) in clarifying and rendering explicit the end of the impulse; (2) in detecting relevant relations between the actual situation and the end; (3) in co-ordinating the various impulses and their systematization into comprehensive purposes. Now, it seems to me that in instinctive activity proper the form of the total series which constitutes the instinctive act is not as such determined by an apprehension of relevant relations. Such partial adaptation and modification of the component parts of the instinct as is occasionally observed may imply no more than an awareness on the sensori-motor level, and is hardly articulate enough to be called intelligence. At what precise point we may speak of intelligence it is difficult to say, but I doubt whether the term ought to be predicated below the level of what Stout calls 'explicit ideas' and Hobhouse 'the practical judgment'. If this line of consideration be accepted it would seem that the statement often made that instinct and intelligence coexist at all stages is not strictly true. It would be better to say that instinct moves between an upper limit—intelligence—which, as it advances, takes its place by substituting articulate apprehension of relations for the mere persistence of impulse and hereditary response, and a lower limit—reflex action—in which nothing but stereotyped behaviour is possible.

On the view here taken, there are present in instinctive behaviour affective elements colouring and qualifying the urge or urges which constitute the core of the instinct. These affective elements, however, are not as such emotional. Emotions in the strict sense are tendencies which come into play in conditions of tension or maladjustment arising from conflict or delay, or failure of normal responses, or suddenness of excitement, or over-stimulation. They are diffuse nervous disturbances arousing varied impulses, with heightened or intensified feeling tone, and generally they pass out of this state of diffuse excitement or 'shock' into adaptive states with characteristic directions of activity. Their function seems to be to sustain interest and to increase the plasticity of behaviour in circumstances in which normal responses fail or are inadequate to relieve excitement or tension. Mr. Shand has shown that their value as compared with instincts lies in (1) the greater force which they bring to bear upon a given situation, (2) their potentially more complex and adaptable systems.[1]

Summing up, we may say that instincts are impulses innately determined to pursue certain ends. In the simplest forms the ends are unforeseen and the patterns of behaviour whereby they are realized relatively fixed and uniform. There appears to be always, however, at least sensori-motor action rendering possible a certain adaptation of the inborn patterns to the requirements of a situation. Instinctive behaviour has unity and persistence and some degree of prospective reference, or forward direction, and this differentiates it from a reflex action. As intelligence develops the ends come more clearly into consciousness, and the relation of the means required for their fulfilment to the ends are grasped more and more articulately. But though the plasticity of behaviour is thereby indefinitely increased, the impulses remain, and the ends of life, however systematized, retain as their central core something of the original impulses. The urge of the instincts has feeling tone, but is not as such emotional, and there does not appear to be the precise relation between instinct and emotion that Professor McDougall claims for the primary instincts.

I propose now to deal with some of the objections that have been raised against the use of the notion of instinct

[1] See Chapter VI.

in psychology and sociology. It has been argued that the notion of instinct involves an appeal to mysterious agencies which is of no scientific value. Prof. Dewey complains, for example, that instinctual psychology is on a level with the stage of physical science in which men spoke of nature's abhorrence of a vacuum, or of a force of combustion, of heaviness, of levity. To explain behaviour as due to hunger, fear, sex, etc., as though they were specific forces, is to indulge in a lazy mythology, and to abandon the real work of tracing connexions and correspondences between mental elements and factors in the environment physical and social.[1] It must be granted that this and similar objections do apply to much that has been written in social psychology where instincts are often invented *ad hoc* to account for all sorts of phenomena, but it does not seem seriously to touch the use of the notion of instinct properly interpreted. The idea of causality as I understand it does not imply any reference to mysterious forces or agencies. Causality is a relation of continuity in changes of character, and in this sense does not require the idea of compulsion or necessity. Perhaps I may be allowed to quote here an illuminating passage from Prof. Alexander. He says: 'The experience we have in our own persons of causality is so far from giving us a notion of mysterious and unexplained efficacy or power that it is but an example of the same relation as we find outside ourselves in external events. Rather we must say that power is the continuous connexion which we observe in ourselves and can more easily and directly observe in ourselves in enjoyment than outside us in contemplated events. Our power is an instance of causality; causality is not the work of power.' In a note he adds: 'Our awareness of power is but our consciousness of the causal relation between our will and our acts. The mischief of the

[1] *Human Nature and Conduct*, Chap. VI.

conception that cause has power to produce its effect is that it introduces some mysterious element of connexion other than that of simple continuity. Hume went too far in the opposite direction.' [1] We ought not, therefore, to speak of instincts as drives or as initiating or producing movements. All that we mean is that amid the antecedents of action are felt impulses whose basis is laid in the hereditary structure and which pass over into overt acts and are such that there is peculiarly intimate continuity in the changes of character of the impulses and the overt acts in relation to the environment. When Dewey further objects that there is not one fear but a thousand fears, all equally original, the objection must be granted to have force. At the same time these different fears have something in common, and if, for example, we can establish that fear is caused by the suddenness, intensity, or unfamiliarity of an impression, we achieve a generalization comparable to generalizations asserting a causal uniformity in the physical world. In this connexion some explanation is required of the significance to be attached to the word tendency or disposition often used in reference to the instincts. Here again we do not refer to vague forces or agencies. Tendencies are part conditions of action or development in the sense that they require to be completed by other part conditions or cause factors to produce given effects. When we say that an animal inherits certain tendencies to behave in a given way, we merely mean that he inherits certain factors which in an appropriate environment will mature and lead to action under appropriate stimulation. The reference of an action to an instinct or instincts is, of course, not a complete explanation ; it merely places the action under the category of inherited equipment, and its further explanation must await fuller knowledge of the factors determining heredity in general.

[1] *Space, Time, and Deity*, Vol. II, pp. 290–1.

Much has been made by some critics of what they describe as the blending and overlap of instincts. Common elements of locomotion, pursuit, and the like are, for example, involved in the instincts of pugnacity, pairing, and food-seeking. The responses, in other words, lack specificity, so that it becomes difficult to say in terms of the overt acts what constitutes ' an instinct '. It must be admitted that specificity is a matter of degree ; even reflex actions are not in the intact organism at any rate now regarded as purely localized responses. Yet in the purer forms of instinct we do speak of specific responses in the sense that they consist of elements of behaviour also found possibly as components of other instincts, yet possessed of what Lloyd Morgan calls ' a relational form ' or peculiar mode of integration characteristic of each instinct. Further, and this is perhaps more important, the objection has no bearing at all on the view which finds the real nature of instinct in specificity of impulse. For a specific impulse may persist throughout a series of activities and integrate them into a distinctive whole, though it may utilize movements which also act in the service of other instincts. The impulse to escape is different from the impulse to fight, though certain movements may be common to both.

Other critics have concentrated upon the wide differences of opinion that exist among psychologists in regard to the classification of human instincts. But I do not know why we should expect prompt unanimity in such a complex matter. It will be found, moreover, that none of the critics succeed in the end in dispensing with the notion of instinct. Prof. Dewey admits that impulses are the pivots upon which the reorganization of activities turns, and that in any study of social change we must go to the analysis of native tendencies.[1]

[1] *Human Nature and Conduct*, p. 98.

Prof. Knight Dunlap restores the expelled instincts under the guise of desires. Even Prof. Bernard protests that there are instincts, possibly even thousands of them. The problem of their classification thus remains in any case.

Having defined the notion of instinct, we may now turn to its applications in social science. It would be clearly impossible to deal even in outline with all the branches of social science in which appeal has been made to the idea of instinct. I will therefore confine myself to certain general lines of reflection which a survey of recent social psychology suggests, and to putting forward certain general criticisms and emendations. In the first place, the work of the last thirty years has brought out the great complexity and intricacy of some of the facts of mental and social life which earlier writers were content to lump together under single headings. A good example of this is to be found in the study of the facts labelled imitation. Tarde, following Bagehot, found the essence of social life in imitation, but he gave very little attention to the psychological analysis of the processes involved. We now realize that there are several different types of imitation. It has been found necessary to distinguish between cases in which the action imitated is one for which there is a prior innate tendency, cases of an almost reflex type, others in which the acts imitated consist of operations not inherited but already acquired by the individual in the course of his previous experience, and others again in which the acts are entirely new. It would seem to be agreed that there is no general tendency to imitate, and that these different types of imitation require each its own explanation. Although there is still much disagreement about these matters, yet much recent experimental work is of a nature which promises a solution of these problems. Another example is the study of suggestibility which is now seen not to be a single specific tendency but to involve different affective-conative factors in different cases.

Perhaps the most important question that arises in connexion with the theory of instinct concerns the manner in which the relation between the inherited disposition and the self is to be conceived. It seems to me that in many of the discussions of this question the essential unity of the mind has been ignored or misinterpreted. The instincts are often represented as separate entities, each with a certain amount of energy of its own. The self is then looked upon as a sort of aggregate of them created by a series of successive integrations. This view, to which the phenomena of conflict and repression gives countenance, leaves unaccounted for the fact that the mind exhibits throughout a tendency to organize its activities and to give them unity of aim and direction. This tendency towards unity of integration is not merely one tendency amongst others, but seems to express something that goes to the root or core of personality, and to be laid down in germ at any rate from the beginning of development. Some have appealed in this connexion to a subject or ego independent of the inherited disposition and controlling its development. This, however, would not seem to be necessary, at least so far as psychology is concerned. The unity of the self need not be sought in a subject existing apart from the states of its manifestation. The self is its states, conscious and unconscious, welded together by a relation of continuity. This continuity is fundamentally conational and is due to the fact that the mind is essentially forward-looking, purposive, dynamic. But the conation is rooted in inherited and permanent needs which act selectively upon the environment and determine the direction of mental development. The stream of mental development has, so to speak, a current whose direction is in part influenced by the inherited structure. The unity of the self is thus one of causal or functional continuity determined by the inherited needs and aptitudes in relation to a varying environment. The selective activity of the inherited disposition is limited (*a*) by the opportunities which the environment, physical and social, affords, and (*b*) by the obscurity and inchoateness of the impulses which are its instruments. Development consists in these being made explicit, and as far as possible harmonious, by a selective handling of the environment within the range open to the individual.

Another result of the development of the psychology of the instincts has been a certain disparagement of reason as a factor in social life and a glorification of impulse. Reason by itself, it is often said, is cold and neutral, and at best can only help in the discovery of means for a realization of ends not of its own making. This seems to me to be based on a false separation between rational will and impulse ultimately to be traced to the lingering influence of the old faculty psychology and the associationist view of the mind which frequently went with it. The instincts and the impulses are regarded as separate entities or ' forces ' competing for mastery with one another and confronted with another entity called reason or will supposed to have no energy of its own, and compelled to borrow its motive power from the sentiments or interests. But this is to ignore the conational unity of the self and to erect a false contrast between the modes of manifestation of the self and the self. In truth, conation and cognition develop *pari passu*, and thought and impulse are inseparably intertwined, and this not merely in the sense that impulse is needed to incite thought, but still more in that thought is needed to clarify and liberate impulse. The assertion that reason is not concerned with ends is mere dogma; we spend half our lives in trying to find out what we want. Impulse is erratic and unstable. Moral reflection is concerned just with the clarification and evaluation of the ends of conduct. Ends, moreover, must not be sharply dissevered from means. Human actions are an integrated whole in which ends and means profoundly affect one another, and it is often impossible to elucidate the one without having due regard to the other. Thought and reason cannot really be expunged from the sphere of conduct. Those who attack it to the glorification of impulse, or action, or the will to power, are inspired by too narrow a view of the function of reason and by a romantic and sentimentally optimistic belief in a pre-established harmony between the demands of impulse and the intricacies and complexities of actual life.[1]

These considerations suggest the need of a restatement of the theory of human motivation implied in much current social psychology. It seems to me that the view that the ultimate motives to action are to be found in the specific impulses which have been called the instincts is misleading. The ultimate drives are to be found rather in what, following Prof. Hobhouse, I should like to call the root interests or basic needs, of which the instincts are differentiations or even limitations. It is true that for some purposes the instincts must be regarded as units. But this merely means that they occasionally exhibit a partial independence from the rest of the personality. It does not mean that they are the ultimate elements of the personality. The basic needs arise out of the relations of the psycho-physical organism to its environment and are integral parts of a rational being. Each primary need is served by specific tendencies of various sorts, but the primary need is the real drive and retains its power of control. Without

[1] cf. Dewey, *Human Nature and Conduct*, Chap. VIII ; and my *Psychology of Society*, Chap. III.

any pretence to completeness they may be grouped as follows:

Root Interests	Specific Forms
Supply of bodily needs.	Hunger, Thirst, Excretion, Exercise, Rest, Sleep, etc.
Needs arising out of man's relation to physical world. Mind making itself at home in the world.	Avoidance of injury. Investigation. Construction.
Needs arising out of relations to other life. Needs of others.	Response and craving for response, specialized in: Dependence, Protection, The sex relation.

The part played by heredity in defining these ultimate needs and providing the means necessary for their attainment varies greatly from case to case. Thus in sex and maternity the innate drives seem to organize behaviour on lines which in general are innately determined. On the other hand, the cognitive and constructive impulses are, in the nature of the case, much more profoundly determined in their mode of manifestation by experience. In this connexion the distinction between emotion and instinct is especially important. Emotion appears to be often contingent and derivative. There is no original or primary need of jealousy, or fear, or anger; they arise in conditions in which other instincts are obstructed or when the normal equipment fails in dealing with a situation. Again, emotions, as Mr. Shand has shown, are much more plastic than instincts and often admit of alternative modes of behaviour. But, though contingent on deeper impulses, they are true racial characters in the sense that they are of generic application and express themselves in acts the basis for which is in general laid down in the hereditary constitution. The wide range of emotional susceptibility is especially to be noted in view of some recent investigations relating to fear made by Dr. Watson. He tries to show that there are very few specific inborn fears. His conclusions are based on controlled observations of infants, among whom he finds that inborn fear is evoked only by loud noises or the sudden withdrawal of support. But surely these specific fears are of very little importance in social life. There are general fears of much wider scope liable to be elicited by any sudden disturbance of the normal routine, by impressions of sufficiently violent intensity rendering difficult immediate adjustment, or by the appearance of a familiar object in an unfamiliar setting or in unfamiliar isolation. We may recall here the example given by William James: 'Any one's heart would stop beating if he perceived his chair sliding unassisted across the floor'—or we may compare Stern's account of his daughter Hilde, aged two years and seven months, who was terrified by a couple of doll's eyes that had dropped out of a broken doll. It is clear that such fears are possible at all levels of life, and indeed lie only beneath the surface of the mind ready to be evoked. The same width of range is characteristic of other emotions, notably anger and anxiety, yet they are innate in our constitution and follow characteristic lines of behaviour. Their expression, varying with changes in the social setting, is a proper object of study for the social psychologist.

A great deal of work remains to be done on the classification of the specific impulses and their relation to the root interests of the personality. Much in recent social psychology seems to me to be vitiated by the effort to deduce from a specific impulse what is perhaps really derivable from a general proclivity of which the specific impulse is only one manifestation. Thus it appears mistaken to derive all knowledge from the instinct of curiosity. This, as a specific impulse to explore and manipulate, is rather one of the ways in which the broader need of the mind to understand, to construct, and appreciate, expresses itself. So again it is a mistake to derive all social behaviour from a specific instinct such as gregariousness, which, if a true instinct in man, is only one form of the broader needs of others which constitute the root interest of sociality. It is possible that what often passes for sublimation is not really the transference of the energy of one instinct to another, but the evocation of another aspect of the root interest involved in the situation. A somewhat similar point arises in connexion with the psychology of morality. Various writers have tried to account for the development of the moral life in terms of an interplay of specific impulses such as submissiveness and assertiveness, resentment and gratitude, and the like. These accounts seem to me one-sided. The growth of the moral life involves an effort to deal with all the elements of our nature, the organization of all the turbulent impulses by the aid of a synthesis adapted to the requirements of social life. The sense of obligation, it would seem, is not to be traced to a specific instinct or instincts, but is the expression in consciousness of the massive organization of all our impulses.

These reflections cannot be here further pursued. It would seem that the chief defect of instinctivist psychology has been its tendency to break up the mind into discrete atomic units. In this it has been and still is greatly influenced by the prevalent theories of the mechanism of inheritance. Scrutiny of these theories will soon show that they have not yet begun to be seriously examined in relation to the inheritance of mental characters. The notion of psychical genes resident in the germ plasm would seem to imply a mechanizing of the mind totally incompatible with the deeper teaching of recent psychology. The theory of mental inheritance ought, in any event, to be based on a direct study of the facts of psychology and not to be deduced ready-made from theories framed on a study of the inheritance of physical characters alone. The whole problem requires restatement in the light of a more adequate definition of the relation between the root interests, the specific impulses, and the complex sentiments and other systems built up in the course of experience, individual and social. There is here a vast field of study calling for the intimate co-operation of psychology and sociology.

VIII

THE INHERITANCE OF MENTAL CHARACTERS

THAT mental traits, whether of intelligence, temperament, or character, have an innate basis is a view which is now very generally accepted. The mind does not start as a *tabula rasa*, but is endowed at birth with potentialities, which no doubt require a suitable environment for their expression or actualization, but which nevertheless set a limit to the attainments of the individual, in the sense that there are certain points beyond which he cannot go no matter how favourable the environment, and in the further sense that the potentialities act selectively upon the environment so that in similar environments some individuals will respond to certain stimuli, while others will remain indifferent to them. So much may be safely said. Not uncommonly, however, we meet with statements both in popular and scientific writings which go a good deal beyond this. Thus, for example, we may be told that mental differences between individuals are due only in a minor degree to differences in the environment, whether physical or social, and are determined for the greater part by inherited factors, or that physical and mental characters are inherited with the same intensity and obey the same laws of transmission. Is there any warrant for such statements ? What do we really know about the laws of the inheritance of mental characters ?

I propose to discuss the evidence as briefly as possible under the following heads : *A*, Pathological traits—for example, feeble-mindedness and insanity. *B*, Exceptional abilities or talents; specific abilities. *C*, Normal characters of intelligence, temperament, and character.

A.—Feeble-mindedness is not so much a medical as a legal or social category, indicating an incapacity of adaptation to a normal environment as judged by certain criteria, which undoubtedly vary considerably and are in the nature of the case more or less arbitrary. It is a condition of suspension of mental development, either congenital or early acquired. In diagnosis it is now usual to employ mental tests, but careful workers take into consideration not only the intelligence level, but also emotional and volitional traits, physical characteristics, and general behaviour. Feeble-mindedness is widely held to be largely hereditary in nature. Some authorities assert that two-thirds of all the cases are so determined. The evidence upon which assertions of this order are based is derived generally from statistical studies, showing that in a large proportion of the cases studied the parents or the siblings of the feeble-minded are also feeble-minded. It is, of course, recognized that mental deficients are not a unitary type, and that some forms of deficiency at any rate are due to an arrest of development caused by various environmental agencies. But it is maintained on strong evidence that many forms are familial in incidence, and these, it is urged, are due to heredity. The problem is whether familial incidence is adequate proof of heredity. Here authorities are divided.

The majority of the studies so far made do not provide control groups for comparison, and there are considerable differences of opinion as to the proportion of feeble-minded in the general population. Even in the cases of family pedigrees, where the proportion of deficients is obviously greater than would be expected from what is known of the general distribution of feeble-mindedness, the studies so far made do not appear to allow sufficiently for the possible influence of a common bad environment. Prof. Morgan says that 'it is quite probable that there are extraneous factors involved in such pedigrees'.[1] A still more formidable point is that, in the opinion of many authorities, even well-authenticated cases of familial amentia are not true germinal variations, but are caused by an injury to the germ plasm, which may affect families for a few generations without being truly hereditary in character. In refutation of such objections family histories are often quoted showing the recurrence of feeble-mindedness during several generations. It is claimed, moreover, that the study of such family records strongly suggests that in many cases the defect is transmitted in an orderly manner indicative of a mechanism and in harmony with established laws of hereditary transmission. Thus, for example, Goddard concludes on the basis of elaborate studies that feeble-mindedness behaves as a recessive Mendelian unit character. From other investigations—those of Reiter and Osthoff—it would appear that it sometimes acts as a dominant and sometimes as a recessive, which is conceivable on the assumption, in itself reasonable, that there are different forms of inherited feeble-mindedness.

These and similar conclusions are often quoted as established truths, but the evidence upon which they rest is extremely dubious and very far from being accepted by many competent students. In the first place, the data, though generally reliable in regard to the children studied in the first instance, in view of the fact that in most recent inquiries they are carefully tested, are far from being trustworthy in regard to the relatives, particularly of past generations, where the evidence is often mere heresay and the diagnosis of no medical value. In regard to Goddard's inquiry, it has been pointed out that, apart from the doubtful value of much of the

[1] *Evolution and Genetics*, p. 201.

evidence relating to ascendants, there are 696 cases out of a total of 1,752 which for various reasons remain unclassified. No one can tell whether the ratio of normals to defectives alleged to be found in the classified group would have been confirmed or not had it been possible to include this comparatively large unclassified group.[1] In the second place, the line dividing the feeble-minded from the normal is for many forms of the defect quite arbitrary, and students of the subject will be familiar with the frequent changes in the standards employed. In the earlier inquiries the lower limit of normality appears to have been much too high. In Goddard's inquiry adults testing twelve years or less were regarded as feeble-minded. Now, the lower limit is taken to be ten or nine years. Quite obviously, this is a serious matter when Mendelian ratios are being calculated. Indeed, the graded character of mental ability and the known facts of the distribution of intelligence make it extremely doubtful whether levels of intelligence as expressed in intelligence quotients can be rightly regarded or treated as units likely to segregate in inheritance. Finally, if we bear in mind the undisputed fact that feeble-mindedness may in many cases be brought about by unfavourable conditions affecting the germ plasm or the foetus *in utero*, statistical results which do not discriminate adequately between the different forms of mental deficiency become still more questionable. The environmentally induced forms ought clearly not to be included in the calculation of Mendelian ratios; but in most cases it is quite impossible, from the nature of the methods employed, to obtain the necessary information. Moreover, many of the studies so far made lump together in their tables all sorts of mental diseases, and even irregularities of behaviour, as judged by some arbitrary standard, and

[1] cf. Ellis, *The Psychology of Individual Differences*, p. 334.

these are then taken as hereditarily equivalent—a procedure which implies a theory of polymorphic inheritance of very questionable validity. In short, whatever our ultimate view may be as to the wider problem of the inheritance of mental deficiency, it is safe to say that it has so far not been proved to behave as a Mendelian unit. It may be well perhaps to quote in support the opinions of a geneticist and a psychiatrist. Prof. T. H. Morgan says: 'Until some more satisfactory definition can be given as to where feeble-mindedness begins and ends, and until it has been determined how many and what internal physical defects may produce a general condition of this sort, and until it has been determined to what extent feeble-mindedness is due to syphilis, it is extravagant to pretend that there is a single Mendelian factor for this condition.'[1] Dr. A. Myerson concludes, after a careful survey, that 'the trend of opinion is certainly away from the conception of feeble-mindedness as a unitary character. Most writers are firmly convinced that there is a familial transference of certain types of feeble-mindedness, and there is very distinctly appearing the view that these familial cases originate in injury to the germ plasm.'[2]

The evidence for the inheritance of the insanities is at first sight more impressive, but closer investigation reveals amazing differences of opinion among authorities, showing that what is really known about it amounts to very little. Among the better documented forms are those of manic depressive and dementia praecox. For the former Kraepelin gives a hereditary incidence of 80 per cent; for the latter 53 per cent. It is to be noted that most of the investigators give no control groups for comparison, nor is the distribution of these diseases in the general population known with any

[1] *Evolution and Genetics*, p. 201.
[2] *The Inheritance of Mental Diseases*, p. 85.

accuracy. It is becoming clear, moreover, that these groups of mental disease are not likely to be idiotypical unities, and that a great deal of classification and psychological analysis of symptoms will be required before specific inheritance, at any rate, can be demonstrated. Recent workers, again, are suggesting psychogenic theories of mental discase which bid fair to revolutionize the older views of the causes involved. Kraepelin himself says that the aetiology of dementia praecox is at present surrounded by an impenetrable fog. Myerson says: 'We have established no pathology for manic depressive or dementia praecox. We have no absolute criteria for their diagnosis. We do not know whether they are a dozen characters rolled into one or whether they are mere diseases.'[1] In regard to causation, some writers deny that heredity has anything to do with it.[2] Others think that the familial form is found frequently in the catatonic group, while in the paranoid group it is met with less often. The large percentages obtained for manic depressive *may* possibly be due, as MacCurdy suggests,[3] to the methods by which information is obtained. As to the applicability of Mendelian laws the best authorities are extremely cautious. Hoffmann says of schizophrenia that Mendelian notions can be applied only with the greatest caution; and Rudin, who has studied large numbers of cases, will commit himself only to the negative statement that as yet no one has a right to say that Mendelian laws do not apply to mental diseases. Even with regard to the main problems of heredity in general we frequently find in psychiatry remarkable changes of front. For example, epilepsy used to be attributed to heredity to the extent of one-third of all the cases. But now authorities are very

[1] loc. sit., p. 284.

[2] cf. Dr. James Kerr, *The Fundamentals of School Health*, p. 411.

[3] *The Psychology of Emotion*, p. 14.

sceptical. French writers assign only a mimimal rôle to heredity,[1] and Myerson tells us that the heredity factor has not been proved to exist.[2] Upon the whole question we may again quote Morgan: 'At best one can say, perhaps, that in certain strains, and perhaps under certain conditions, mental disorders appear; but so long as neither the physiological background of insanity nor the external agents that are contributory are known its genetic relations must remain obscure.'[3] We may conclude that, though it is well established that a good deal of insanity is familial in incidence, very little appears to be known with regard to the intensity of inheritance or the relative rôle of inborn and environmental factors.

B. In the study of the inheritance of exceptional abilities or talents Galton's famous work on *Hereditary Genius* is still regarded by many as fundamental. Essentially his method consisted in showing that among the relatives of eminent men, such as judges, statesmen, literary men, scientists, artists, and divines, there were found individuals who have attained distinction, in numbers far larger than was to be expected on the assumption that superiority or distinction was distributed in the population regardless of inheritance. Thus the 300 families which he studied contained 977 eminent men, of whom 415 were of especial distinction. He showed that on the average 100 famous men had 31 eminent fathers, 41 eminent brothers, 48 eminent sons, 17 eminent grandfathers, and 14 eminent grandsons. These figures have often been quoted, but the really important figures are those given by Galton in column E of his table, which takes into consideration the total number into whose relationships he inquired,

[1] cf. Poyer, *Les Problèmes Généraux de l'Heredité Psychologique*, p. 137.

[2] p. 72.

[3] *Evolution and Genetics*, p. 203.

including those famous men who had no eminent relations. The figures given for the judges are: fathers 9·1; brothers 8·2; sons 12·6.[1] For the other categories he does not provide tables, but suggests a method for obtaining column E,[2] on certain assumptions. This gives as the chance of kinsmen of illustrious men attaining eminence as 15·5 to 100 in the case of fathers, 13·5 in the case of brothers, and 24 in the case of sons. In other words, the chance of the father is 1 to 6; of each brother 1 to 7; of each son 1 to 4. From this he concludes that qualities making for eminence run in families. He further claims to show that the influence of heredity is closely related to the degree of kinship, the intensity of inheritance diminishing in a regular manner at each successive remove, whether by descent or collaterally. Thus in the second grade the chances are of each grandfather 1 to 25; of each uncle 1 to 40; of each grandson 1 to 29. In the third grade the chance of each member is about 1 to 200, except in the case of first cousins, when it is 1 to 100. It will be remembered that this second result came to be formulated more precisely in the law of ancestral inheritance.

Of the many difficulties inherent in this procedure attention is here drawn only to the more important. Firstly, Galton's estimate of the proportion of eminent men is based upon a consideration of the number of men who attain success as judged by the attention they secure in dictionaries of biography, obituary notices in *The Times*, and the like. Those who are familiar with the methods by which these matters are managed will not be greatly impressed with such criteria of inborn superiority. It is to be remembered, further, that dictionaries of biography are apt to concentrate on distinction in the world of literature, science, and politics to the comparative neglect of other spheres of activity, in which

[1] p. 55. [2] p. 312.

a great deal of ability may yet exist which thus fails to get recorded. In the second place, the fact that the relatives of successful men have a greater chance of attaining eminence than others is of course susceptible of explanation in environmental terms. Galton dismisses such explanations on the ground that genius is irrepressible and will secure expression despite untoward circumstances. His arguments, though eloquent and persuasive, are not convincing. The investigations of Odin, de Candolle, and Cattell have shown, by methods similar to those employed by Galton, the importance of suitable environmental conditions in the expression or realization of faculty. Finally, perhaps the most important objections to taking Galton's results as a measure of the intensity of inheritance may be derived from the teaching of modern genetics as it has developed since his work. Johannsen has convincingly shown that Galton's laws are not strictly biological laws, but merely statistical generalizations relating to outward resemblances in highly mixed populations, from which but little can be inferred as to actual inborn constitution without a great deal of further analysis.

Galton himself did not attempt to analyse in any detail the constituent elements which go to the making of the complex 'talents' whose distribution he investigated. Since his time it has become increasingly clear that talents are very complex 'constellations' of numerous elements united and correlated into wholes. It seems probable that in most cases the correlation is the result of repeated trial and not part of the original endowment, and it is possible that in unfavourable circumstances the requisite combination or correlation is not achieved. It may be added that the whole question of the relation between special and general factors in mentality is at present hotly debated. There would appear to be no satisfactory evidence of the inheritance of special abilities when they have been investigated by modern methods.[1]

C. We may now turn to some representative investigations into the inheritance of normal mental characters. Perhaps the most influential has been that conducted by Prof. Karl Pearson. In 1904 he obtained by means of a questionnaire the ratings of teachers of about 3,000–4,000 siblings in various English schools in regard to certain physical qualities, such as eye colour, hair form, cephalic index, and a number of mental qualities —viz. vivacity, assertiveness, introspection, popularity, conscientiousness, temper, ability, and handwriting. He found that siblings resembled one another in respect of these qualities to an extent which he expresses mathematically by a mean coefficient of correlation of about ·5. This figure has since been widely taken as a measure of heredity, and has been used as a starting-point for further deductions, relating, for example, to the influence of the environment.[2] There are, however, various difficulties which I will briefly discuss. To begin with, the data in respect of the mental qualities were derived from the subjective estimates of teachers. It has been shown experimentally that such estimates are subject to errors of surprising magnitude.[3] This is especially important in view of the complexity of some of the qualities under investigation, and the probability that the standards employed may have differed widely from place to place. Moreover, the figure ·5 measures resemblance ; but this, Prof. Pearson argues, cannot be explained as due to similarity in the environment in which brothers and sisters are brought up, on the ground that a similar figure is obtained in respect of certain

[1] cf. Starch, *Educational Psychology*, p. 83 seq. ; and Hazlitt, *Ability*, Chap. V.

[2] cf. Carr-Saunders, *Eugenics*, p. 88.

[3] cf. Prof. Spearman, *Eugenics Review*, 1915, p. 230.

physical qualities, such as eye colour in which environmental influence is excluded. 'If the environmental influence is the same in the two cases it is insensible, for it cannot influence eye colour. If it is not the same, then it would be a most marvellous thing that, with varying degrees of inheritance, some mysterious force always modifies the extent of home influence until the resemblance of brothers and sisters is brought sensibly up to the same intensity.' May we not reasonably invert this argument and ask whether it is not a marvellous thing that, if the figure ·5 really expresses the intensity of hereditary factors, it should turn out to be the same for definitely measurable qualities like head height and vaguer and more complex qualities like health, the same for eye colour and intelligence, and within the range of mental characters for qualities of such varying complexity as conscientiousness and ability, introspection and popularity? Other investigators, it may be added, find by no means the same amount of resemblance in siblings in respect of emotional or temperamental traits as they do in respect of intelligence; and, though the differences in the results may be due to defects in methods of testing, yet it would seem on the whole very improbable that subjective estimates of outward resemblance in respect of qualities so complex and so varied in nature should in all cases have hit upon the hereditary factors involved.

Without pursuing these difficulties any further, we may turn to studies of the resemblance between siblings which have been made on the basis of mental tests instead of teachers' estimates. There is now quite a large number of such investigations, and owing to the different tests employed their results are difficult to compare. Miss Elderton, using Dr. Kate Gordon's material, arrives at a coefficient of ·467. In another inquiry she gives a coefficient of ·669 for one school and

·394 for another. Pintner, using six different tests, gives a coefficient of ·22. Thorndike, with three different tests, gives ·29, ·30, and ·32. Starch, employing various tests, gets an average of ·42. Miss Hildreth's correlations vary from ·27 to ·68. Mr. R. A. Davis obtains ·24 to ·54 with the Dearborn tests and ·15 to ·55 with the Haggerty tests. Generally the coefficients for pairs of unrelated children cluster round zero. The resemblance in mental qualities between siblings appears thus well established by these investigations, but they do not appear to have substantiated the claim that there is a constant correlation of ·5, and they leave quite undecided the question as to whether the resemblance is due to heredity or to similarity in home and other environmental conditions. To overcome this last difficulty various devices have been employed by students. Here reference can be made to only some of the more important. Thus the resemblance in intelligence of siblings brought up in orphanages has been studied with the object of eliminating differences in home environment, but in most studies so far reported the children did not spend the earlier years of their lives in the institution, and it is arguable that it is just those years that are of the greatest significance in influencing development. Of greater importance, perhaps, are the studies that have been made of the mentality of twins. It has been shown that they resemble one another to a much higher degree than do other fraternal pairs. Thorndike tested fifty pairs of twins, and found a coefficient ranging from ·70 to ·90. Merriman, in an extensive investigation, finds a coefficient of about ·80. Twins that are physically similar resemble one another more closely in intelligence than do other twins. Like-sex pairs resemble another more closely than unlike-sex pairs, whose degree of similarity approaches that of ordinary siblings. The following results may be quoted in illustration: For like-sex pairs Merriman finds a coefficient of ·84; Wingfield gives ·82 and Lauterbach ·57 for all mental traits, and ·77 for intelligence. For unlike-sex pairs the same investigators give ·59, ·59, ·33, and ·56 respectively. The facts suggest that the increasing degree of resemblance is closely related to increasing degree of genetic affinity.

Recently several investigations, more or less successful, have been made into the inheritance of qualities of temperament and character. Of these the most interesting perhaps are those of Hoffmann, who bases his results on clinical experience and on detailed and intensive analysis of family histories. He has sought tentatively to apply Mendelian ideas to his material. But his results and those of others working on similar lines must at best be regarded as very provisional. There are well-nigh overwhelming difficulties in such investigations. The existence of mental characters has to be inferred from outward behaviour, but the motivation of acts is extremely complex, and the same outward behaviour may be due to quite different motivating influences in different cases. For example, 'timid' behaviour may be due in one case to excessive development of innate fear; but it may also be the result of inhibitions or a feeling of inferiority due to the particular history of the individual. In the second place, there is as yet no good working classification of qualities of temperament and character, and very little knowledge of the relation of the various qualities to one another, nor any agreement as to which are to be regarded as primary and which as derivative. How, for example, are sociability and intolerance related to the feeling of inferiority? How are qualities of temperament related to intelligence? Does it not often happen that when the need for self-expression, hitherto inadequate, receives satisfaction, intolerant and unsociable indeviduals become or appear sociable and tolerant? In the third place, the whole notion of mental units is extremely difficult to interpret and to relate to the underlying unity of personality. It is hardly credible that the complex qualities so far studied can behave as Mendelian units, and psychological analysis will have to advance a great deal before the methods of genetics can be profitably applied in this field. It remains to be added that so far no working hypothesis has been suggested of the way in which the inheritance of mental characters is to be conceived. It is true that heredity is in any case a mystery. The history of genetic theories in recent times shows that the factorial hypothesis, which at one time seemed straightforward, has had to be supplemented by a host of subsidiary hypothesis, such as polymeric inheritance, incomplete dominance, variable valency of factors, linkage and repulsion of factors and the like, to a degree which strongly suggests that the time is perhaps ripe for a complete revision of the whole theory. But the difficulties are vastly enhanced when the conception of factorial units is applied to mental qualities. The notion of psychical genes resident in the germ cells would seem to imply a mechanizing and atomizing of the mind hardly in harmony with the teaching of modern psychology.

Upon the whole, we may conclude that the cumulative effect of the evidence is to suggest that heredity plays a rôle in determining individual differences in mental characters, even though we must insist with T. H. Morgan [1] that at present there is 'no real scientific evidence of the kind that we are familiar with in other animals and plants'. Allowance must of course be made for the inevitable difficulties of investigation when human material is in question. But this must not obscure the plain fact that as yet there is no accurate quantitative knowledge of the laws governing the

[1] *Evolution and Genetics*, p. 206.

inheritance of mental traits, nor any plausible hypothesis of the manner in which such inheritance is to be interpreted. For the claims of those who pretend to measure with precision the relative rôle of inborn and environmental factors in mental development there appears to be no scientific warrant whatever.

IX

INTERCHANGE BETWEEN SOCIAL CLASSES

DESPITE the important rôle which the idea of social class has played both in social theory and in political movements, very few scientific studies exist of the nature of class differentiation and its conditions. Marx and his followers have sought to relate the various forms of social stratification to modes in the forms of production, but it would seem on an inadequate inductive basis, at any rate as far as modern conditions are concerned. In recent times efforts have been made, under the influence of biological ideas, to determine the relation between forms of social groupings and differences in physical and mental characters between individuals and groups. These are held to afford material for the agencies of social selection and thus to influence social differentiation in greater or lesser degree. But studies on these and other lines have suffered from the absence of an adequate classification and the lack of agreement with regard to the criteria of class, which makes effective comparison of the results arrived at by different investigators extremely difficult and precarious.

The difficulties of classification are due, among other things, to the fact that social differentiation is psychologically conditioned, and that as yet there exists no generally accepted technique for the observation, analysis, and record of the behaviour of social groups in relation to one another. When psychological analysis has been attempted at all, it has generally been in the direction of determining the ends or interests which classes have in common, with the result that writers have tended to deny the reality of class distinctions or to minimize them, in cases in which it was not possible to point to definite cohesive groups clearly aware of their interests as groups. But social classes are not associations to be defined by their ends or purposes, but groups of individuals related to one another by much vaguer, though not less powerful psychological attitudes, and which only under certain conditions come to be conscious of a class purpose. It is extremely difficult to say what one is conscious of when one is class conscious, but the following psychological factors would seem to form part of the situation. There is firstly a 'feeling of kind' as it may be called, in relation to members of one's own class, a confidence that one can meet them on equal terms. There is, secondly, a feeling of inferiority in relation to those above in the hierarchy, and, thirdly, a feeling of superiority in relation to those below. All these states of mind, which psychologists would interpret in terms of the theory of 'sentiments', are extremely complex, partly because of the large number of gradations in the social hierarchy, the continual intersection of levels in mobile societies, and partly because the sentiments of equality, inferiority, and superiority admit of subtle and intricate forms of inversion and compensation. *Prima facie* the determinants of these feelings and attitudes are to be found in differences in mode of life, educational standing, amount and intimacy of association between members of different groups, and the various factors, political and economic, which make for confidence and assertiveness on the one hand and submissiveness and negative self-feeling on the other. It must be confessed that scientific sociologists have hardly even begun to study these matters, which are often treated with greater insight by novelists and essayists.

In the present investigation [1] I have endeavoured to deal with a small portion of this large question by seeking to obtain a measure of the degree of movement between social classes, the reality and importance of the 'social ladder'. In what is no more than a preliminary inquiry, I have had to content myself with taking fairly readily identifiable groups, namely, those which are indicated by mode of occupation, on the ground that from the latter may generally be inferred a person's mode of life and educational standing and therefore his social class, if we understand by this term a group of people who meet one another on equal terms. I have distinguished the following categories:

Class I. includes professional, employers I, own account I.

Class II. includes employers II, own account II, salaried.

Class III. includes wage-earners, skilled, semi-skilled, and unskilled.

I found subsequently that my classification coincided very largely with that adopted by the Registrar-General.[2] He distinguishes five social grades: I, Upper and Middle. 2, Intermediate. 3, Skilled. 4, Intermediate. 5, Unskilled. The details supplied in the Report referred to have been a great assistance to me in dealing with my data. These include:

A. Information derived from answers to a Questionnaire.

B. MS. records of admissions to Lincoln's Inn.

C. Information derived from Prof. Bowley's investigations into the social conditions of five towns.

[1] I am greatly indebted to Mrs. Cressmann (*née* Loch) for her invaluable and untiring assistance throughout this laborious piece of work. Thanks are also due to Mr. J. Rumyaneck, who helped me in the initial stages of the inquiry.

[2] *Decennial Supplement*, Pt. II, 1921.

A. The Questionnaire [1]

This was circulated in the years 1927–8 among university teachers and students, teachers in training colleges, second-class civil servants, clerks, and other salaried officials and wage-earners. They were asked to state their occupation, i.e. the kind of work they did, and their employment, i.e. whether they were employers or working on their own account, and if they were working for others whether they were salaried or wage-earners, and to supply similar information relating to their fathers, grandfathers paternal and maternal, brothers and sisters if working. The following table shows the occupational range and sex distribution of those who filled in the form :

	Total	Women
Student group	580	252
Teachers group	872	537
Professional	113	21
Employers I	2	—
Employers II	29	1
Own account II	33	5
Salaried	765	88
Wage-earners	450	27
	2,844	931

[1] I wish to thank the following for their kind co-operation in the circulation and collection of the questionnaire forms : The Principals of Avery Hill Training College ; the London Day Training College ; the Diocesan Training College, Bristol ; the Training College, Darlington ; St. Peter's College, Peterborough ; Whitelands Training College, London ; the Provost of University College, London ; the Principal of King's College, London ; the Organizing Secretary of the Extension Board, University of London ; the Students' Union of the London School of Economics ; Mrs. H. Reid of Bedford College, London ; Prof. J. E. Neale ; Miss Monkhouse ; Mr. Arthur Pugh of the Iron and Steel Trades Confederation ; Mr. A. G. Walkden of the Railway Clerks' Association ; Mr. C. T. Cramp of the N.U.R. ; Mr. William C. Keay of the Federation of Professional Workers ; Mr. R. H. Tawney.

The principal results are set out in Tables I–VI.

TABLE I

Comparison of Present Generation and Father's Occupation

PRESENT GENERATION

		Professionals	Students	Employers I	Independents	Employers II	Own Account II	Salaried (Miscellaneous)	Salaried (Teachers)	Wage-earners	Totals
FATHERS	Professionals	35	164	1	—	—	1	38	62	3	304
	Employers and Own Account I	9	16	1	—	1	—	6	8	—	41
	Independents	2	2	—	—	—	—	1	—	—	5
	Employers II	20	109	—	—	15	5	91	170	20	430
	Own Account II	8	43	—	—	2	10	77	73	61	274
	Salaried	28	171	—	—	3	—	182	249	37	670
	Skilled	7	69	—	—	6	12	276	246	180	796
	Semi-skilled	3	3	—	—	1	3	58	46	115	229
	Unskilled	—	—	—	—	—	—	17	4	20	41
	TOTALS	112	577	2	—	28	31	746	858	436	2,790[1]

TABLE II

Comparison of the Occupations of Fathers and Paternal Grandfathers

FATHERS

		Professionals	Employers I	Independents	Employers II	Own Account II	Salaried	Skilled	Semi-skilled	Unskilled	Totals
PATERNAL GRANDFATHERS	Professionals	141	8	1	14	10	25	7	—	—	206
	Employers and Own Account I	12	9	1	6	1	8	2	—	—	39
	Independents	9	1	1	2	1	7	3	—	—	24
	Employers II	49	14	2	243	56	126	90	11	4	595
	Own Account II	21	4	—	56	105	109	137	32	3	467
	Salaried	34	4	—	32	17	145	43	8	—	283
	Skilled	11	—	—	38	39	136	288	52	10	574
	Semi-skilled	6	—	—	7	11	35	94	92	8	253
	Unskilled	1	—	—	2	2	3	12	4	7	31
	TOTALS	284	40	5	400	242	594	676	199	32	2,472

[1] It will be observed that the totals in these tables differ. This is due to the fact that many of the forms contained incomplete or indefinite entries, with the result that several had to be altogether omitted, while some, though utilizable for certain tables, were not available for others.

Table III

Comparison of the Occupations of the Fathers and Maternal Grandfathers of the Present Generation

FATHERS

		Professionals	Own Account & Employers I	Independents	Employers II	Own Account II	Salaried	Wage-earners: Skilled	Wage-earners: Semi-skilled	Wage-earners: Un-skilled	Totals
Maternal Grand-fathers	Professionals	93	8	—	26	8	35	8	—	—	178
	Employers I and Own Account I	21	5	—	4	4	6	2	—	—	42
	Independents	3	2	1	8	1	9	6	—	—	30
	Employers II	84	13	3	169	55	161	92	14	4	595
	Own Account II	18	3	—	39	78	96	119	31	5	389
	Salaried	36	3	—	39	23	127	57	12	2	299
Wage-earners	Skilled	17	2	—	62	52	129	263	50	7	582
	Semi-skilled	3	—	—	23	22	26	106	77	6	263
	Unskilled	—	—	—	—	1	3	8	8	6	26
	Totals	275	36	4	370	244	592	661	192	30	2,404

Table IV

Table comparing the Occupations of Paternal and Maternal Grandfathers

PATERNAL GRANDFATHERS

		Professionals	Employers and Own Account I	Independents	Employers II	Own Account II	Salaried	Skilled	Semi-skilled	Unskilled	Totals
Maternal Grand-fathers	Professionals	69	8	4	46	16	17	7	1	—	168
	Employers and Own Account I	20	7	2	6	3	3	2	—	—	43
	Independents	6	5	3	1	6	2	1	—	—	24
	Employers II	58	10	6	254	78	60	83	11	3	563
	Own Account II	12	2	1	52	‘133	33	92	29	3	357
	Salaried	22	5	3	61	53	67	64	5	1	281
Wage-earners	Skilled	5	2	3	77	98	52	195	90	9	531
	Semi-skilled	1	—	1	35	41	10	66	86	7	247
	Unskilled	—	—	—	3	4	2	10	3	4	26
	Totals[1]	193	39	23	535	432	246	520	225	27	2,240

[1] *Note.*—For the purposes of this table the following forms have been omitted:

(i) All forms in which the occupations of the Fathers of the present generation have not been given.

(ii) All forms in which the occupations of the Paternal Grandfathers of the present generation have not been given.

(iii) All forms in which the occupations of the Maternal Grandfathers of the present generation have not been given.

(iv) Queried (i.e. indefinite) forms for both Grandparents. For detailed numbers of omissions see Tables V and VI.

TABLE V

Table Comparing the Occupations of the Present Generation with that of their Paternal Grandfathers

PRESENT GENERATION

		Professionals	Students	Employers and Own Account I	Employers II	Own Account II	Salaried: Miscellaneous	Salaried: Teachers	Wage-earners	Totals
PATERNAL GRANDFATHERS	Professionals	30	100	2	1	2	32	39	3	209
	Independents [1]	2	9	—	—	1	3	10	2	27
	Employers and Own Account I	9	14	—	1	—	4	9	1	38
	Employers II	31	157	—	8	3	157	209	33	598
	Own Account II	12	90	—	8	13	142	119	87	471
	Salaried	11	81	—	3	—	74	100	16	285
Wage-earners	Skilled	7	87	—	2	9	162	187	126	580
	Semi-skilled	3	13	—	2	1	88	45	102	254
	Unskilled	1	3	—	—	—	10	4	13	31
	TOTALS	106	554	2	25	29	672	722	383	2,493

TABLE VI

Table Comparing the Occupations of the Present Generation with that of their Maternal Grandfathers

PRESENT GENERATION

		Professionals	Students	Employers and Own Account I	Employers II	Own Account II	Salaried: Miscellaneous	Salaried: Teachers	Wage-earners	Totals
MATERNAL GRANDFATHERS	Professionals	18	89	1	2	4	29	34	1	178
	Employers and Own Account I	9	21	1	—	—	6	5	1	43
	Independents [1]	2	7	—	1	—	10	9	1	30
	Employers II	44	157	—	12	1	154	193	37	598
	Own Account II	12	66	—	3	11	134	88	80	394
	Salaried	11	86	—	1	2	67	115	19	301
Wage-earners	Skilled	7	97	—	3	2	171	183	124	587
	Semi-skilled	5	19	—	1	4	76	69	93	267
	Unskilled	—	1	—	—	—	7	1	17	26
	TOTALS	108	543	2	23	24	654	697	373	2,424

[1] No Independents in present generation.

In order to facilitate comparison I have grouped the subdivisions into three classes and expressed the results in percentages. Class I corresponds to the Census division Upper and Middle and includes professionals, students, employers I, own account I and independents. Class II corresponds to the Census division intermediate II and includes employers II, own account II, salaried officials, elementary school teachers. Class III includes the working class and corresponds to the Census divisions, skilled, intermediate and unskilled.

MOBILITY OF OCCUPATION TABLES

Tables in Percentages

Table I

Comparison of the Occupations of the Present Generation with those of their Fathers

PRESENT GENERATION

		Class I	Class II	Class III
Fathers	Class I .	33·3	7·0	0·69
	Class II	54·9	52·7	27·1
	Class III	11·9	40·2	72·3

Table II

Comparison of the Occupations of Fathers and Paternal Grandfathers of the Present Generation

FATHERS

		Class I	Class II	Class III
Paternal Grandfathers	Class I .	55·6	6·0	1·3
	Class II	38·9	71·9	36·2
	Class III	5·5	22·1	62·5

Table III

Comparison of the Occupations of Fathers and Maternal Grandfathers of the Present Generation

FATHERS

		Class I	Class II	Class III
Maternal Grandfathers	Class I .	42·2	8·4	1·8
	Class II	50·8	65·3	38·1
	Class III	7·0	26·4	60·1

Table IV

Comparison of the Occupations of the Paternal and Maternal Grandfathers of the Present Generation

PATERNAL GRANDFATHERS

		Class I	Class II	Class III
Maternal Grandfathers	Class I .	48·6	8·2	1·4
	Class II	46·7	65·2	37·7
	Class III	4·7	26·6	60·9

TABLE V

Comparison of the Occupations of the Present Generation with those of their Paternal Grandfathers

PRESENT GENERATION

		Class I	Class II	Class III
PATERNAL GRAND-FATHERS	Class I .	25·1	7·0	1·6
	Class II	57·7	57·7	35·5
	Class III	17·2	35·2	62·9

TABLE VI

Comparison of the Occupations of the Present Generation with those of their Maternal Grandfathers.

PRESENT GENERATION

		Class I	Class II	Class III
MATERNAL GRAND-FATHERS	Class I .	22·7	7·2	0·80
	Class II	57·6	55·9	36·5
	Class III	19·8	37·0	62·7

The tables show that 12 per cent of the present generation in Class I had parents in Class III, the corresponding figure for the last generation being 6. If one generation is omitted and the present generation compared with the grandparental the figure is about 18. It should be noted that those classed as 'professionals' in the present generation include numerous students whose future occupation is indeterminate. The movement from Class II to Class I is naturally greater. The results may be summarized thus :

UPWARD MOVEMENT

	From III to I	From II to I	From III to II
Present generation and fathers . . .	12	55	40
Fathers and grandfathers	6	45	24
Present generation and grandfathers . .	18	57	36

The downward movement may be measured by ascertaining the proportion of those at present in the lower classes who originated in the upper. The figures are as follows :

DOWNWARD MOVEMENT

	From I to III	From I to II	From II to III
Present generation and fathers . . .	0·6	7	27
Fathers and grandfathers	1·5	7	37
Present generation and grandfathers . .	1·4	7	35

The proportion who remain in their own class is indicated in the following table:

	I	II	III
Present generation and fathers . . .	33	52	72
Fathers and grandfathers	48	68	61
Present generation and grandfathers . .	23	56	62

In considering these figures it may be useful to bear in mind the estimate made by the Registrar-General of the proportion of the classes distinguished by him per cent of the occupied population.[1]

All Classes	I	II	III	IV	V
100	2·93	20·35	43·47	20·45	13·40

Some indication of the extent of intermarriage between the groups in the grandparental generation may be obtained from Table IV. It will be seen that in Class I, 4 per cent of the maternal grandfathers were wage-earners. In Class III only 1·4 were professional, while the corresponding figures for their own class and for Class II were fairly even, viz. 48 and 46.

Upon the whole, the following conclusions suggest themselves. There is evidence of upward mobility from Class III to Class I, and this seems to be increasing

[1] cf. Registrar-General's *Decennial Supplement*, Pt. II, p. viii.

as compared with the past generation. This does not bear out the view that the process of recruiting talent from the lower classes to fill the gaps in the upper has reached a point of exhaustion.[1] Further, on the evidence before us there is very little downward mobility from I to III, and this is not in harmony with the suggestion often made that the lower classes are recruited sensibly from the failures of the upper.[2] Bearing in mind the proportion of the classes in the occupied population, it is indeed evident that the ladder can only lift relatively small numbers. There seems thus little ground for the hypothesis of 'drainage' and no indication that the reserves of ability in the lower classes are being depleted.

B. Admissions to Lincoln's Inn [3]

I have endeavoured to obtain information regarding the social strata from which the professions are recruited, but the only case in which I have obtained reliable data related to the legal profession as judged by the entries to Lincoln's Inn. The following table shows the occupations of the parents of those who were admitted to the Inn between the years 1886–1927 (with two breaks, 1894–1903 and 1912–18).

It will be noted that there is on the whole but little change in the proportions in which the different classes contribute to the entries in the period reviewed, except that there is some decline in the contribution made by the clergy in recent times and that there are signs of the working class beginning to creep in.

[1] cf. McDougall, *National Welfare*, p. 162.
[2] cf. Sorokin, *Social Mobility*, p. 457.
[3] I wish to thank the Treasurer and Governing Body of Lincoln's Inn for their kind permission to copy the MS. records of admissions to the Inn.

TABLE A

Table (in Percentages only) of the Occupations of the Fathers of those admitted to Lincoln's Inn between 1886 and 1927, except for the years, 1894–1903, and 1912–18. Total Admissions, 1,268. (This total does not include foreign or colonial students nor those apparently brought up abroad).

Period Covered	Class I[1] 'Upper and Middle'						Class II Intermediate			Class III	Average *Present Age* of those Admitted
	Legal Professions	Clerical Professions	Other Professions	'Gentlemen'	Employers I	Own Account I	Employers II	Own Account II	Salaried[2]	Skilled Wage-earners	
1886–9 . . . *216* Admissions	22·7	14·4	20·8	23·2	6·5	0·46	8·3	0·93	2·8	—	65–56 years of age
1890–3 . . . *215* Admissions	28·8	14·4	15·4	20·5	7·9	0·93	10·7	0·47	0·93	—	61–57 years of age
1904–8 . . . *255* Admissions	22·4	9·8	15·7	33·3	2·4	0·78	12·2	—	3·1	0·40	48–45 years of age
1909–13 . . . *173* Admissions	18·5	6·9	27·8	17·9	4·6	2·3	11·6	0·58	9·8	—	46–38 years of age
1919–22 . . . *190* Admissions	20·0	10·0	20·0	27·4	4·7	1·6	8·4	2·6	4·7	0·53	37–33 years of age
1923–7 . . . *219* Admissions	25·6	3·7	24·7	17·8	8·2	3·7	9·6	0·92	4·1	1·8	31–25 years of age

TABLE B

Table (in Percentages only) of the Occupations of the Fathers of the Benchers of the Middle Temple, between the years 1886–1912.

No. of Benchers	Class I					Class II			Class III
	Legal Professions	Clerical Professions	Other Professions	Employers and Own Account I	'Gentlemen'	Employers II	Own Account II	Salaried	Wage-earners
76	22·4	11·8	11·8	13·2	23·7	13·2	2·6	1·3	—

[1] The Classes used are those employed in the Census.
[2] This category includes teachers, other than University Teachers.

C. Professor Bowley's Data

My third set of data is derived from the cards which Professor Bowley kindly put at my disposal giving information of the social conditions of working-class populations in five towns compiled in the surveys made by him in 1924. The occupations of the workers have been classified into the five main categories employed by the Registrar-General. The nature of the occupation rather than the rate of wages has been regarded throughout as the basis of classification. This has been observed as much in the case of young workers as in the case of adults, and apprentices to skilled trades have been reckoned as skilled, whatever their wage-rates. The high wages paid to labourers as compared with those paid to skilled men in many cases made such a method necessary. Female workers have been graded on the same basis as men as regards skill, e.g. a woman weaver or cotton spinner has been graded as skilled without reference to the difference in payment between male and female weavers and spinners.

Of the many interesting points suggested by these tables attention may be drawn to two. Firstly the proportion of children of the working class rising to Class II varies from 4 per cent from the unskilled parent to 10 per cent from the skilled; whilst that rising to Class I is on this information negligible. Secondly, the notion that the unskilled form a stable group is not borne out by these figures, in view of the fact that only 18 per cent of their children remain in that class, the bulk going to the skilled. These conclusions are subject to the qualification that the cards gave information only of the children who lived at home at the time of the survey and that the classification was in many instances difficult.

Occupations of Male *Children compared with those of their Fathers, in 1924. (Bolton, Northampton, Reading, Stanley, Warrington)*

	Father's Social Class	Class V. Unskilled Children	Class IV. Inter-mediate Children	Class III. Skilled Children	Class II. Inter-mediate Children	Class I. Upper and Middle Class Children	Total No. of Children
Whole Numbers	Unskilled V . . Total 270	81	52	130	14	1	278
	Intermediate IV . Total 254	45	82	130	13	—	270
	Skilled III . . Total 673	95	85	433	59	3	675
	Intermediate II . Total 49	4	2	22	20	—	48
	Upper and Middle-Class . . . Total 2	—	—	4	—	1	5
	TOTAL 1,248					TOTAL	1,276
The same Table in Per centages only.	Unskilled V . .	29·1	18·7	46·7	5	0·37	278
	Intermediate IV .	16·7	30·4	48·2	4·8	—	270
	Skilled III . .	14·1	12·6	64·2	8·7	0·45	675
	Intermediate II .	8·3	4·2	45·8	41·7	—	48
	Upper and Middle-Class . . .	—	—	80	—	20	5
						TOTAL	1,276

Occupations of Children compared with those of their Fathers for Five Towns in 1924. (Bolton, Northampton, Reading, Stanley, Warrington)

Father's Social Class.	Class V Unskilled Children	Class IV Inter-mediate Children	Class III Skilled Children	Class II Inter-mediate Children	Class I Upper and Middle Class Children	Total No. of Children
Unskilled V . . . Total 270	18·1	24·0	53·7	4·0	0·19	520
Intermediate IV . . Total 254	11·2	32·8	49·8	6·3	—	464
Skilled III . . . . . Total 673	8·3	16·8	64·7	10·0	0·25	1,225
Intermediate II . . Total 49	5·3	5·3	51·3	38·2	—	76
Upper and Middle . Total 2	—	—	83·3	—	16·7	6
TOTAL 1,248					TOTAL	2,291

Taken together with the conclusions suggested under the previous sections they confirm the view that the social ladder so far lifts only relatively small numbers. The results derived from the three sets of data are not, of course, comparable. B. and C give information referring to two generations only, whilst A deals with three. B concerns only one branch of a single profession and C is an almost exclusively working-class sample, while A covers all classes. Yet the results so far as they go are not incongruent. The conclusions relating to the movement between Classes II and III and between II and I are not stressed, as the classification is difficult. In dealing with the more clear-cut distinction between Class I and Class III, it should be borne in mind that in C we are estimating the proportion of working-class children who rise, whilst in A we estimate the proportion of people at present in Class I who originated in Class III, and remembering the proportions of these classes in the general populations the conclusions seem compatible. It would seem that there has been an increase of mobility upwards in the present generation, whilst the downward movement is slight and nearly constant during three generations.

X

THE CLAIMS OF EUGENICS

EUGENICS may be defined in the words of Galton as the science of the agencies under social control which may improve or impair the racial qualities of future generations. As so defined there can be no doubt of its importance. Whatever view we may take of the nature of civilization and of the forces which bring about social change, we must admit that the genetic constitution of the stock which is the bearer of civilization is a matter deserving of study. The inclusion of the notion of social control in the definition has perhaps its dangers. It tends to obscure the distinction between pure and applied science, which in this case is of especial importance. While in animals and plants experimental breeding on an empirical basis is completely justified both on practical and scientific grounds, in dealing with human beings it has to be borne in mind that to justify social control we need a great deal more than a merely rough empirical knowledge of heredity, and indeed more than a scientific genetics. We need to know the broader social effects of selective breeding, and we need ethical and aesthetic standards of value by the aid of which we could decide what to breed for. In short, applied eugenics requires not only genetics but sociology and social philosophy. A survey of eugenic literature suggests very strongly that this requirement has been overlooked, with the result that biological conclusions, well or ill founded in themselves, have been used as the basis for practical policies, which could be justified, if at all, only after elaborate sociological and ethical study.

In essentials the eugenic position may be summed up in the following propositions:

(i) That individual differences in mental and bodily characters are determined mainly by heredity and only to a very small extent by environment; that 'nature dominates nurture'.

(ii) That progress depends upon natural selection.

(iii) That modern conditions are tending to suspend the selective death-rate, while, on the other hand, 'they have allowed prepotent birth-rate to be associated with a tabid and wilted stock'.

(iv) That consequently degeneration has set in and must continue unless measures are taken to counteract the evils that arise from the suspension of the selective death-rate and the present contra-selective or cacogenic birth-rate.

I propose to deal with these propositions *seriatim.* With regard to the first, it may be taken as highly probable that in the main the mechanism of inheritance which has been established for other forms of life will be shown to operate also in man. There is already good evidence of the applicability of the main Mendelian processes, such as simple dominance and recessivity, sex linkage, and the like, to the bodily characters of man. The inheritance of mental characters is also highly probable, though an examination of the evidence shows as we have seen (see Chapter VIII) that at present practically nothing is known of the laws of their transmission, and there is no recognized hypothesis of the way in which such transmission is to be conceived. The main proposition that the mental and bodily characters of man have a hereditary basis need not be disputed. We must, however, deny that it has been shown either that mental characters are inherited in the same way or with the same intensity as physical characters, or that the influence of the environment is slight or negligible. The former point need not here again be stressed as it has already been discussed in the chapter above referred to. With regard to the latter, the view that the bodily differences among men are due to genetic factors is widely held, but this is not to say that the comparative unimportance of environmental factors has been shown. A large number of investigations undertaken by the Biometric school do indeed purport to show that only a negligible association exists between bodily characters and various environmental variables. But these investigations have given rise to much controversy—often unnecessarily acrimonious—and though their precise value cannot yet be estimated, it is clear to me that they do not justify the assumption, tacit or explicit, of their conclusiveness, so frequently made in eugenic writings. A few examples of these investigations may be briefly referred to in illustration. Prof. Pearson concludes that the alcoholism of parents 'has practically no influence on the general health and intelligence of boys and girls, and the little influence it has is in favour of the children of drinking parents, they are healthier and more intelligent'.[1] But the investigations upon which these startling conclusions are based can be effectively criticized, as it seems to me, on the ground that the data were not representative, that many of the accounts were based on the merest hearsay evidence, that it was not clear that the factor of alcoholism had been effectively isolated from other possible factors, and especially that there was little information as to whether the parental alcoholism occurred before or after the birth of the offspring.[2] It may be added that other investigators

[1] *Relative Strength of Nature and Nurture*, p. 18.

[2] cf. J. M. Keynes, *Jour. Royal Stat. Soc.*, 1910, p. 773; and Newsholme, *Vital Statistics*, p. 548.

have arrived at contrary results. Thus Laitinen and Legrain find a definite relation between the weight and health of children and alcoholism of parents.[1]

Somewhat similar remarks apply to the conclusions reached by the Biometric school regarding the relation between alcoholism and mental defect. The results reached in the different investigations are not in themselves quite consistent, but in any event the data are regarded by specialists as of doubtful value. Dr. Myerson in a trenchant examination of the biometric work describes the criteria employed for judging mental defect 'as fit to make a psychiatrist weep'.[2]

The need for caution in accepting the conclusions as to the relative insignificance of environmental factors reached by this school is especially obvious, as it seems to me, in their treatment of infant mortality. They hold that inborn factors—nature value—are at least 4·5 times more important than environmental conditions —nurture value—as tested by conditions like overcrowding, dampness, possibility of ventilation, and, more generally, that infant mortality is highly selective. That there is some selection is probable. Constitutional equipment must of course count, and this is confirmed by the correlation that has been shown to exist between parental longevity and low infant mortality. Yet, on the whole, medical evidence assigns a preponderant influence to environmental factors in determining the magnitude of infant and child mortality. It is true that it has proved difficult to establish a definite correlation between any one environmental factor and infant mortality. But this is due to the complexity of the environmental influences and their intricate intermingling. Broad relations between the environment and infant mortality are clearly visible.

[1] cf. Elster, *Sozialbiologie*, p. 412.
[2] *The Inheritance of Mental Diseases*, p. 39.

Infant mortality varies enormously in different countries, and even in different regions in the same country or districts in towns. Thus, for example, for the years 1901–5 the mortality rates for 1,000 births were:

Austria	213	Belgium	148
Hungary	212	France	139
Germany	199	England	138
Spain	173	Switzerland	134
Italy	167	Sweden	92
Serbia	149	Norway	81

The following table gives the infant mortality rates per one hundred births in different countries for 1923:[1]

Egypt	14·3	Denmark	8·5
Rumania	20·6	New Zealand	8·9
Bulgaria	10·9	Scotland	10·1
Japan	16·8	Norway	5·4
Spain	14·2	Germany	13·2
Hungary	18·6	Irish Free State	6·8
Italy	15·8	Belgium	10·7
Danzig	16·0	Switzerland	7·0
Netherlands	5·7	France	9·6
Finland	9·9	England and Wales	6·9
Austria	15·6	Sweden	6·3

In each country extreme variations may be shown to exist in different districts or parts, and even in different wards of the same towns. In England, Newsholme has shown that 'in a very high proportion of towns in any part of the country, the rate of infant mortality in one part of a town may be 50 or even 100 per cent higher than that experienced in another part of the same town.[2]

[1] *Stat. Jahrbuch für das Deutsche Reich.*, 1924, p. 11.
[2] Second Report, p. 20.

Very considerable differences exist also in the death-rates of infants under four weeks. 'They varied from 19 per 1,000 births in Oxford to 56 in Barnsley, from 43 in the aggregate rural districts of Middlesex to 109 in those of Durham.'[1] In American cities infant death-rates in the first month have been shown to vary from 34 to 54 per 1,000 births.[2] The precise causes of these variations remain to be ascertained, but they are hardly likely to be found in differences in innate characters.

Infant mortality varies also in a striking manner with social class, as will be seen from the following table : [3]

	RATE IN 1911	RATE IN 1921
I. Upper and Middle . . .	76	38
II. Intermediate	106	55
III. Skilled Workers . . .	113	77
IV. Intermediate	122	89
V. Unskilled Workers . .	153	97

It may be added that the increase of mortality from Class I to Class V is more marked in the later sections of the first year of life, and since the deaths in the earliest periods are the least preventable, this strongly suggests that the later deaths are largely caused by remediable adverse environmental conditions.[4]

Upon the whole, the very wide variations in infant mortality, and the rapid changes which have occurred in its rate of incidence, are hardly to be accounted for in terms of genetic variability, and suggest the enormous importance of environmental factors, despite the fact that no satisfactory methods have yet been devised for disentangling the numerous variables involved. Upon

[1] Registrar-General, 1920, p. xlii.
[2] *American Journal of Hygiene*, Vol. III, May 1923.
[3] *Decennial Supplement*, 1921, p. xcvi. [4] cf. ibid., p. c.

the whole question I may perhaps quote the verdict of Sir Arthur Newsholme: 'The relatively insignificant place given by the correlation method to environmental conditions is so contrary to the experience of medical officers for health, which shows the great improvement securable in an infantile population by the application of personal, domestic, and municipal hygiene, that one must suspect the validity of the tests used in the investigation or the method employed in isolating them from other factors.' [1] In general the impression left by the studies of the Biometric school is that the failure to detect the influence of the environment is more likely to be due to the inadequacies of method and the indefiniteness of the data than to the non-existence of the influence.

I turn now to the second proposition, which assigns to selection a preponderant rôle as an agent of progress. 'Selection,' says Prof. Pearson, 'is the sole effective process known to science by which a race can continuously progress. The rise and fall of nations are in truth summed up in the maintenance or cessation of that process of selection.' [2] This thesis is widely held by eugenists, yet I am not aware that they have even made a beginning in the elaborate ethical and sociological investigations that would be required to substantiate it. It is doubtful whether even in biology it is correct to speak of natural selection as a cause of progress. Without entering here into the highly controversial question of the rôle of selection in evolution, it will be generally conceded that selection is not an originative agent but at most an instrument of preservation or perpetuation. The causes of variation are completely unknown, and it is they alone, whatever they may be, that could claim to be regarded as agents of change, progressive or other.

[1] *Vital Statistics*, p. 546.
[2] *Groundwork of Eugenics*, p. 20.

In any event, in dealing with social evolution, we need direct evidence that social changes are determined by natural selection, and ought not to rely upon biological arguments, which at best could only have the force of analogy. When the facts of social life are studied directly it becomes clear that the factors bringing about change differ *toto coelo* from those which are supposed to operate in the field of biological evolution, that human quality does not differ profoundly from period to period, and that progress is in the main independent of changes in genetic structure, but depends upon changes in tradition and on methods of adaptation and organization increasingly independent of specific race qualities. I have discussed this at some length in Chapter IV, and will not repeat the arguments there adduced. But attention must be drawn to the remarkable fact that while in biology the hypothesis of selection has recently been subjected to close scrutiny, and quantitative evidence of genetic variation, elimination and survival is insisted upon, writers on social evolution are content to invoke selection without undertaking the necessary investigations into the nature of human variability and into the relation between survival and genetic factors. A good example of what I have in mind may be found in the use frequently made of the notion of selection in dealing with war. In order to make the notion applicable it would be necessary to show (i) that war between groups results in the substitution of one genetic type for another, that is to say, in the expansion of the conquering people and the diminution or elimination of the conquered ; (ii) that the elimination and expansion are achieved on the basis of genetic characteristics belonging to the groups at war. Unless there is elimination and unless the elimination is grounded in genetic variability, there can be no selection. On neither of these points do biological discussions of war ever supply any satisfactory evidence. It is by no means clear that war results in most cases in the numerical diminution of the conquered. The common view—for example that the contact between the white and the coloured peoples has led to the extermination of the latter—is in the majority of instances completely unfounded. On the contrary, the expansion of the European peoples has been associated generally with an enormous increase of the populations of the invaded areas.[1] Nor is ground ever given for the belief that the victors gain their ascendancy because of inborn superiority. The superiority is inferred from success in war, which in turn is then explained by it. In the absence of independent evidence of inborn racial differences such explanation is merely a verbal circle. The relation between acquired technique and training and inborn gifts is not examined. Nevertheless it is obviously of the first importance in a study of the selective effects of war.

Even more unsatisfactory from the point of view of method are the biological explanations of the so-called rise and fall of nations in terms of natural selection. The 'decay' of Rome has been ascribed to the effects of race mixture (Chamberlain) excessive inbreeding (Reibmayr), and the 'extermination of the best' through war and the failure of the ruling classes to reproduce themselves in sufficient numbers (Seeck, Schallmayer, and others). But to begin with, it is by no means clear that there was decay in any biological sense. The racial composition of the 'Romans' is obscure.[2] The term 'best' as applied to the upper class in Rome is question-begging. 'We cannot appraise,' says Prof. Heitland, 'with any approach to

[1] cf. 'The Expansion of Europe,' by F. W. Wilcox, *American Economic Review*, 1915: 'The net result of the expansion of Europe has been an enormous increase in the aboriginal population of the lands to which they have gone' (p. 745).

[2] cf. Ridgeway, *Who were the Romans?*

exactitude the social value of the upper class.' [1] The arguments for any racial decay do not stand investigation. 'The old families,' Hobhouse tells us, 'that made the republic may have died out, but the literary complaints of degeneracy familiar in Horace date, if they have any scientific value at all, from the beginning of the Principate, which was not an age of decadence but of remarkable progress maintained for nearly two centuries. The republic was in decadence since the battle of Pydna, while the great republican families were still flourishing, and if under the empire these families were submerged, there were plenty of vigorous stocks in Italy and the provinces which supplied a succession of able emperors and generals from Trajan downwards. The empire never lacked able men down to the age of Stilicho and Aetius, not to say that of Belisarius or Narses.' [2] Not only is there no evidence of true racial decay, but it is becoming doubtful whether we can correctly speak of a decay even in a cultural sense. Rostovtseff at any rate concludes that the term 'decay' or 'decline' is unfair and misleading. What happened was there was political disintegration, associated with a great change in economic and social life and a gradual shifting in the standards of values. To form a scientific estimate of the nature of the transformation that occurred and its place in the history of civilization, we should have to consider whether the creation of the Roman empire was a good thing for the human race and whether its disintegration was in the long run detrimental to civilization. We should have to weigh up the contributions of the rising Christian Church and the new developments in the field of art. In short, the problem is one not of biology but of history, sociology, and social philosophy. The assertion that the rise and

[1] *The Roman Fate*, p. 55.
[2] Hobhouse, *Social Development*, p. 313.

fall of nations are due to selective process is mere dogma, not only incapable of biological proof but clearly out of harmony with the recent work of the economic and social historians of the ancient world.[1]

The points in eugenic theory that remain to be here discussed may be briefly summed up thus: (i) That the improvement in living conditions due to the growth of 'civilization' and the ameliorative measures of modern social legislation constitute an interference with the 'old selective death-rate' and must result in the progressive deterioration of the race; (ii) that owing to the differential fertility encouraged by modern conditions of life there is occurring a process of reproductive selection which results in the increasing recruitment of the population from the least 'fit' portions of the stock. The logical consequences of the first of these propositions are hardly ever faced by eugenic writers. If it were really true that the destruction of the less fit is 'a beneficent factor of human growth', and 'the chief cause of the mental and physical growth of mankind in the past', there would be a definite cleavage between ethics and biology, a cleavage demanding the entire reconstruction of social and ethical theory instead of a grudging admission that we 'have to take social customs as we find them'[2] But is the situation really so desperate? Must the triumph of mankind, to use Prof. Pearson's phrase, really be built on the martyrdom of men? We have seen that the precise part played by selection in the evolution of species is still in dispute, but even if it be accepted as a principal agent, it is by no means clear that the establishment of new variants is only possible under unfavourable circumstances.

[1] cf. Rostovtseff, *Social and Economic History of the Roman Empire*; 'The Decay of the Ancient World' (*Economic History Review*, Vol. II, No. 2); W. E. Heitland, *The Roman Fate* (1922), *Iterum* (1925), and *Last Words on Roman Municipalities* (1928).

[2] *Groundwork of Eugenics*, p. 39

In human societies in particular it may well be that the emergence of types to which value is attached is only possible in circumstances in which brute struggle is curtailed and a chance of survival given to those whose qualities are not of the obviously ' useful ' type. Moreover, and this seems to me a fundamental point, a great many causes of injury and death are indiscriminate in incidence, and affect the fit and unfit alike. It is at least probable that social and hygienic measures, in removing or restricting such causes of disease and death, confer a benefit upon mankind which must on the whole outweigh the bad results conceivably brought about by enabling some of the constitutionally unfit to survive. In any event, purely deductive arguments as to what ' must ' happen on the hypothesis of natural selection are worth very little. Empirical evidence of racial deterioration as a result of interference with natural selection is not forthcoming. Of English conditions at any rate the Committee on Physical Deterioration, which investigated the matter before the war, concluded that there was no ground for the belief that there was any general physical deterioration, and Sir Arthur Newsholme, reviewing the evidence of the medical boards during the war, concludes ' that the figures do not justify a pessimistic view of English physique. They show the presence of much disease and many defects in a considerable portion of the adult population ; but there is little, if any, reason for thinking that the proportion of these conditions has increased in the last twenty years '.[1] With regard to the problem of mental and nervous degeneration I will content myself with citing the opinion of Prof. Oswald Bumke,[2] who has considered all the available evidence. He says[3]:

[1] Vital Statistics, p. 554.
[2] *Kultur und Entartung*, 1922.
[3] p. 91.

'We know nothing definite about the number of psychically abnormal persons or about the question whether this number has increased or decreased.' And again: 'That there has been an increase in mental disease has not been proved, and in any case such an increase cannot have been large.'[1]

Regarding the relation between fertility and social and economic status there is now a considerable body of information for most Western countries. In general, in recent times at any rate, effective fertility declines with rise in social status. The data at our disposal do not as yet enable us to determine with any certainty how long this variation in the distribution of fertility has been going on, or whether it is likely to continue. In his discussion of the data derived from the Census of 1911 Dr. Stevenson attempted to trace the earlier history of differential fertility back to 1851, and suggests that 'if the comparison could have been carried twenty years further back a period of substantial equality between all classes might possibly have been met with'. On the other hand, a comparison of the figures for 1911 and 1921, given by the Registrar-General, reveals a tendency for the decline in the birth-rate to be equalized—at any rate so far as the divisions within the working classes are concerned. (See Table on p. 188.)

For other countries there is some evidence that the differences in fertility between the social classes are in process of disappearing. Thus an inquiry in Bremen showed that while the births per one hundred inhabitants in 1901 were 1·27 for wealthy districts, 2·89 for middle class districts, 4·37 for the artizan zone, and 4·62 for the mainly labouring class districts, the rates for 1925 were 1·47, 1·42, 1·95, and 1·89 respectively. In Stockholm and Berlin, according to recent reports, the differences have disappeared. There is much in the

[1] p. 107.

data which have so far been collected which strongly supports the view that, in the main, social differences in fertility are not due to genetic but to social and economic factors, and that there is an increasing tendency for the influences making for a lowering of the birth-rate to permeate the lower social grades; but the whole question clearly needs further investigation both from the point of view of the geneticist and the sociologist.

Legitimate Births per 1,000 Married Males under Fifty-five Years of Age

Social Class	Rate in		Rate per cent for all Classes		Rate in 1921 per cent. of that in 1911
	1911	1921	1911	1921	
1. Upper and Middle .	119	98	73	70	82
2. Intermediate . .	132	104	81	74	79
3. Skilled Workers . .	153	141	94	100	92
4. Intermediate . .	158	162	98	115	103
5. Unskilled Workers .	213	178	131	126	84
All Classes . . .	162	141	100	100	89

We must next deal with the consequences of differential fertility, supposing it to be more than a passing feature in Western civilization. It is clear that it cannot be healthy for any society to replenish itself increasingly from those portions of the population which live under the least favourable circumstances. But the evils thus arising are to be met by securing a more equitable distribution of wealth and a general raising of the standard of life among the poor. They are evils socially conditioned and they require remedies of a social nature.

The question, however, remains whether there are any genetic differences in physical and mental characters between the social classes likely to affect the future inborn quality of the stock. The evidence which has been accumulated in this connexion is of very unequal value, and only a brief account can here be given.

Since the pioneer inquiry by the Anthropometric Committee of the British Association in 1880–3 a great deal of evidence has been amassed in various European countries and in America of the relation between social or occupational status and height and weight. Though the results are not strictly comparable they generally reveal a difference of two to five inches for the years six to thirteen (age for age) as between the children of the working classes and the professional and well-to-do classes, the difference being less marked in adults. The interpretation of the results is extremely difficult. *Prima facie* the differences would seem to be nurtural in the broad sense of the word. It may be remarked that Galton favoured this view.[1] Prof. Pearson, on the other hand, thinks that selective factors are involved, men of inferior physique being forced into the lower occupations, and in this he seems to have the support (somewhat qualified) of Prof. Carr Saunders, who thinks that the differences are ' in the main almost certainly inherited differences '.[2] That there is some occupational selection on the basis of physique is probable, but there is no quantitative information of its range or intensity. It is generally held now that stature is in the main determined by hereditary factors, but there is nothing in genetic theory to show that environmental influences are unimportant in the determination of differences in height within the same race. On the other hand, there is some empirical evidence suggesting strongly that

[1] *Inquiries into Human Faculty*, p. 16.
[2] *Eugenics*, p. 128.

height may be affected by changes in the environment. A striking instance of improvement in stature correlated with improvement in the conditions of life which has almost the character of a crucial case may be cited from the work of Bolk.[1] He shows that in the eastern part of Overysel flourishing industries have sprung up during the last thirty years, whilst the western part has remained agricultural. The population of the two parts is racially identical and only very little immigration has taken place into the industrial region, the workers being drawn from the immediate neighbourhood. Bolk shows that in the non-industrial group the number of undersized (—155 cm.) varies from 7 to 9·5 per cent, whilst a height of 170 cm. is only reached by 22·3 to 28 per cent. On the other hand, in the more favourable conditions of the industrial regions the proportion of undersized varies from 1·5 to 2·5 per cent and the proportion reaching 170 cm. from 42·3 to 51·2 per cent. Closely similar phenomena are to be observed in Noord-Brabant. Further, there is evidence that American-born children of Italian and Russian parents are four or five inches taller than their parents, except among the very poorest, where national habits and modes of feeding are retained longer.[2] Boas has noted on the basis of a study of 2,300 cases that while the coefficient for resemblance between parents and children in the case of East European Jews settled in America was ·36 for head length and width, it was only ·21 for height.[3] The influence of environmental conditions upon the height and weight of children is also brought out clearly by the conditions in Germany resulting from the blockade, when the children of all classes were affected equally.[4] and in

[1] *Zeitschrift für Morphologie und Anthropologie*, 18, 1914.

[2] Kerr, *Fundamentals of School Health*, p. 29.

[3] *Zeitschrift für Ethnologie*, 1913, p. 624.

[4] cf. *Deutscher Verein f. öffentliche Gesundheitspflege*, 1921, Heft 6, II.

Russia during 1921–2,[1] where a considerable fall was noticed in the heights and weights of children. The study of primitive peoples also occasionally furnishes evidence of the influence of the conditions of life on bodily size. Thus Torday has shown that certain Congo Batua Pygmies near the Kasai River who left the forest two generations ago and took to a settled agricultural life have attained to a stature far superior to that of the average Pygmy, though not equal to that of the Bushongo neighbours, with whom intermarriage is out of the question.[2] Again, the improvement in the mean stature of Europeans during the last hundred years to the extent of six to ten cm. is usually attributed to improvements in mode of life. It is to be noted peoples of different race but living in a similar environment have benefited alike. In Holland, for example, the difference in the average height of the non-Jewish population for the period 1850–1900 is 10·9 cm., while the Jewish population improved to the extent of 6·3 cm. during the same time. These and other similar facts suggest that for every race there is probably a maximum or optimum height which is reached under favourable conditions, but is depressed in unfavourable ones. Within the same race it is thus quite probable that minor differences in height are of the nature of phenotypical fluctuations. It may be worth adding that the differences in height in different economic grades are most marked in early childhood (though not apparently at birth),[3] and there seems direct evidence that in earlier years factors other than heredity affect the growth of children of both sexes. The correlations

[1] Ivanovsky, 'Physical Modification of the Population of Russia under Famine' (*Amer. Jour. Physical Anthropology*, 1924).

[2] cf. Haddon, *Races of Man*, p. 9.

[3] 'Child Life Investigations' (*Medical Research Council Special Report Series*, No. 81).

obtained between the stature of parents and the stature of children in an inquiry made in Dundee in 1926 are definitely below those obtained by Pearson for adults (son to father r. = ·0448 ± ·047; son to mother r. ·0207 ± ·026; daughter to father r. ·0375 ± ·045; daughter to mother r. ·0758 ± ·205 [1]), which suggests that though the precise nature of the environmental agencies affecting growth cannot yet be determined with certainty, they are of importance at any rate in the early years of childhood.

Apart from stature the physical traits which have been investigated most in relation to social status are head-form and size and cranial capacity.[2] These investigations generally purport to show that the leading rôles in society are taken by long-headed types. I do not propose to deal with these in detail. The facts are difficult to disentangle. Class differences are in European countries and elsewhere evidently complicated by factors due to ethnic intermixture and conquest. It is therefore likely that in some countries the upper classes possess characteristics dominant in the conquering race. But it does not follow that the long-headed types always belong to the upper and professional classes. In Italy, for example, Dr. Livi has shown that in the north the professional classes are longer headed than the peasants, while in the south the opposite rule prevails. In Sweden, apparently, there is a greater percentage of brachycephaly, according to Nystrom, among the educated and upper classes than in the lower. The differences are as likely to fall one way as the other. Their significance is in any event difficult to interpret. There appears to be no significant relation between head form or size and intelligence, or any other mental

[1] *Medical Research Council Special Report Series*, No. 101, p. 110.

[2] cf. Ploetz, *Sozialanthropologie, Kultur der Gegenwart*, III.

trait, and unless we start with assumptions of the racial superiority of one or other type, there is no ground for assigning selective value to these anthropological traits. Lenz [1] cites an investigation made by Matiegka in Prague purporting to show differences in brain weights between members of different economic grades:

14	Unskilled Labourers	1,410 g.
34	Skilled Workers	1,434 g.
14	Servants	1,436 g.
123	Tradesmen	1,450 g.
28	Non-academic Brain-workers	1,469 g.
22	Academically Trained Brain-workers	1,500 g.

But the numbers are small; only averages are given, with no indication of the variation within each class, or of age, stature, nutritional and pathological conditions. I have myself collected information on this subject from the records of the London Hospital in 1929 and obtained the following results (pathological conditions excluded): [2]

106	Unskilled and Labourers	48·81 oz.	± 4·21
136	Skilled Workers	49·08	± 4·49
67	Shopkeepers, Clerks and superior Skilled	49·14	± 4·52
13	Professionals	49·06	± 3·87

So far as they go, these figures do not support Lenz's contention. It should be remembered, further, that there is no reason for believing in any close correlation between crude brain-weight and intelligence, and little significance attaches to the results.

[1] *Menschliche Auslese*, p. 66.

[2] I am indebted to Prof. Turnbull for his kindness in putting the data at my disposal and to Dr. E. Miller for valuable help in classification.

We may next consider the relation between social status and mental characters. So far as I know, there is no evidence relating to qualities of character and temperament. Numerous inquiries have, however, been made both in Europe and America regarding the distribution of intelligence as measured by mental tests such as the Binet-Simon or its modifications. The method followed has been (i) to correlate the intelligence of the children within the same school or schools with the occupations of their fathers; (ii) to compare the intelligence of the children of schools of the same type but situated in different districts from which the economic level of their parents can be inferred; (iii) to compare the intelligence of the children of different types or grades of school in which the children are normally recruited from different social levels. The broad results of some of these studies may be cited. Duff and Thomson made an extensive survey of the school population of Northumberland in 1923 (13,419 children aged 11 and 12), and classified them according to parental occupation. The average intelligence quotients proved to be as follows:

Professional	Shopkeeping	Metal-workers	Low Grade Occupations
112·2	105·0	100·9	96·0

Haggerty and Nash (1924) examined 8,688 children of the ages 9–14 and found the following median intelligence quotients:

Professional	Business	Skilled Workers	Semi-skilled	Farmers	Unskilled
116	107	98	95	91	89

In an earlier inquiry made by Hofman in Breslau in 1912 the children of different types of schools were compared. It was found that the mental age of the 7- and 9-year-old *Volkschüler* was half a year below that of the *Vorschüler*; while the 10-year-old *Volkschüler* had the same mental age as the 9-year-old *Vorschüler*.[1] It may be noted that the results are congruent even if different tests are employed. Thus in the following table the Pressey tests were employed in the Indiana studies and the units were the percentages of children above the median score for their ages; in Columbus the figures give the coefficient of mental ability based on the Yerkes Bridges Point Scale; in Madison the figures give the intelligence quotient based on the Dearborn and National Intelligence Tests:[2]

	Indiana	Columbus	Madison
Professional	83	1·42	114
Business	66	1·26	104
Skilled Trades	47	1·22	97
Unskilled Labour	39	·83	89
Farming	27	—	94
Number Tested	1,206	228	2,782

In estimating the bearing of these investigations upon the problem of genetic differences between the social classes, the following points seem worthy of consideration: (i) There is very little agreement among psychologists as to what exactly it is that the intelligence tests

[1] cf. Stern, *Die Intelligenz. der Kinder und Jugendlichen*, 1920.
[2] cf. *Scientific Monthly*, 1924.

test, but hardly any one would now maintain that they enable us to measure inborn faculty uninfluenced by environmental factors, in the broad sense. Reference may here be made to the 'Report on Psychological Tests of Educable Capacity (1924)', which emphasizes the need of caution in drawing conclusions as to inborn capacity from tests applied to children drawn from widely different environments. (ii) The differences between the occupational groups are small compared with the individual differences within each group. There is, that is to say, much overlapping. In Duff and Thomson's inquiry, for example, the coefficient of association is only 0·28. (iii) Examination of the tests employed shows that generally the children of the economically superior parents do better just in those matters in which their experience at home would help them. In Prof. Burt's inquiry the two social groups differ most in those qualities that 'might be deduced from the peculiar environment and peculiar tradition in which the two groups live and move'.[1] Similarly, in Hofman's inquiry it is clear that the children of the superior school excel in those tests which depend upon the kind of information, mental stimulus, and width of interests associated with the more cultured homes. (iv) There appear to be differences in the rate of growth or development between the children of different economic grades, and in many instances delay in development is made up later by an extra spurt in favourable conditions. Many of the inquiries show that the correlation of intelligence with social status declines with age. Other studies show different degrees of correlation at different ages. The explanation is probably to be found in different rates of maturation, in the fact that the tests for the higher ages are beyond the cultural horizon of the poorer children, in the economic

[1] *Mental and Scholastic Tests*, p. 198.

conditions which compel the brighter children of the poor to leave school for work at an age unduly young, in the equalizing tendencies of schooling and the greater common environment away from home at the higher ages. These factors would operate in different directions and probably account for the discrepancies in the results. They point, however, to the influence of environmental agencies upon the differences observed between the social groups. (v) In some of the inquiries (e.g. Bridges and Coler) the correlation of intelligence and social status is higher for boys than for girls. This suggests environmental factors as has also been noted in the parallel case of race differences. (vi) There is direct evidence from the study of foster-children of the possibility of affecting the intelligence quotient of children by an improvement in the conditions of life. Freeman [1] computes the average gain in intelligence quotient due to the conditions of the foster home as 7·5 points, and Burks [2] estimates the average gain to be about 5 or 6 points. Pintner [3] concludes that the average gain to be expected from a change in the environment at an early age may be from 10 to 20 points. In view of these indications the difference observed between children of different social grades are too slight to be taken as reliable evidence of inborn variation.

The experimental evidence of genetic differences between the social classes is thus far from conclusive.[4] Further progress in this direction depends upon the discovery of more accurate methods for discriminating between the environmental and inborn factors affecting mental development. Eugenic writers, however, do not confine themselves to the discussion of the direct

[1] *Twenty-seventh Year-book National Study of Education*, 1928.
[2] Ibid.
[3] *Foundations of Experimental Psychology*, 697.
[4] cf. Dr. Evelyn M. Lawrence, 'Intelligence and Inheritance' (*British Jour. of Psychology Monograph Supplements* XVI).

evidence of the kind hitherto examined. Far more commonly they take social and economic status itself as an indication of inborn quality. It is supposed that in the social struggle for existence aptitudes find their proper level, that a process of occupational selection occurs whereby the less well-endowed are either eliminated or prevented from reaching the higher social or economic grades, while, on the other hand, men of ability belonging to the lower ranks frequently rise to higher positions, thus enriching the biological quality of the upper grades while impoverishing the lower. The result of this kind of selection it is held, is that on the whole the well-to-do classes represent the abler stocks, and along the whole scale of social life there is an important relation between success and inborn fitness. In dealing with these arguments we must admit the reality of a certain amount of selection. It is clear, for example, that in many of the professions there are minimum requirements of physique or mentality which are enforced by examinations or other tests, so that there is a great deal of weeding out from among those who are financially or socially in a position to enter for them. It should, however, be remembered that failure to qualify for a particular profession on the part of the well-to-do but rarely results in a change of class, but merely involves generally a transfer to some other occupation within the same social status. Further selection is limited to those who enter. But there are undoubtedly vast numbers who have the requisite aptitudes but never get the chance of a trial of strength. The professions are still largely closed to the children of the poor. While the proportion of children estimated as capable of benefiting from higher education is estimated as between 50 and 75 per cent, only about four or five per 1,000 ex-elementary school children reach a university. Such opportunities as are now given to the children of the poor frequently depend upon accidents of place of residence and other factors, which operate with very little regard to qualities of ability and character. It should be remembered further that while in the professions there will be found a certain small proportion of those who have risen from the lower economic grade, the mass of the individuals in the lower grades must necessarily remain where they are.[1] The social ladder can only lift relatively few. It is difficult to see how the rise of a few individuals can affect in any substantial degree the quality of the larger mass.

Of the operation of the social ladder within the working classes, and as between them and the employing classes, very little is known with any accuracy. It appears, however, from the few studies that have been made, whether abroad or in England, that the movement is slow and that very few rise more than a few grades. Numerous instances can no doubt be quoted of employers who have risen from the ranks, but bearing in mind the ratio of wage-earners to employers in the occupied population, it is clear that those who rise form but an insignificant fraction of the total number of wage-earners. In conditions of restricted mobility and initial inequalities of wealth and opportunity it is difficult to see how there could be any close correspondence between inborn faculty and economic position. The superior advantages of inherited wealth must conceal or counterbalance a great deal of native inferiority in the more prosperous classes, while, on the other hand, much ability in the lower classes, owing to lack of stimulus and opportunity frequently gets no chance to express itself. The distribution of income, it may be added, bears no relation to the probable distribution of intelligence or other mental traits ; and it is significant that incomes from property are distributed much more

[1] cf. Chapter IX.

unevenly than incomes from either head-work or hand-work.[1] Upon the whole question more information is needed with regard to (i) the type of physical and mental qualities best adapted to different occupations; (ii) the factors determining choice of occupation; (iii) the extent of interoccupational mobility and the factors affecting it; (iv) the influence of the types of economic structure upon the distribution of incomes; (v) the relative importance of environmental and genetic factors in the moulding of human characteristics, mental and physical.

It remains to be added that in so far as success in the social and economic struggle is determined by individual differences, the qualities in question are not all socially desirable or deserving of admiration. Differences in physical strength, fatiguability and endurance, specialized aptitudes, intelligence must to some extent act selectively in so far as they are not masked by initial inequalities of wealth and opportunities for training. But equally important are such characteristics as assertiveness, pushfulness, greed for power, indifference to the suffering of others, narrowness of sympathy, callousness, the determination to succeed at all costs, with its consequent limitation of interests. On the other hand, gentleness, tolerance, broadmindedness, strength of affections, width and delicacy of taste might well stand in the way of the climber in the business or professional world. We have no means of telling how these qualities are distributed in the different social classes, nor to what extent they are innately determined.

The principal conclusions which emerge from this part of our discussion may now be briefly stated:

(i) The social classes differ at present in their rate of reproduction.

[1] cf. Pigou, *Economics of Welfare*, p. 610; and especially Watkins, *The Growth of Large Fortunes*.

(ii) It is uncertain how long this difference has existed and whether it is likely to continue, and there is some evidence of tendencies to equalization by the spread of the decline of the birth-rate to the lower social grades.

(iii) It is clearly undesirable for the poorest portions of the population to have the largest families on the ground that the children must suffer through being brought up under the least favourable conditions. To the extent to which the decline in the birth-rate is brought about by deliberate limitation, the remedy here lies in securing greater economic equality among the social classes, for the evidence goes to show that the policy of birth limitation is more readily adopted by those who have a decent standard of life to maintain.

(iv) Whether the existing differences in fertility are likely to affect the inborn constitution of the stock depends upon whether there are genetically based differences among the social classes. No satisfactory methods have yet been discovered for disentangling the environmental from the inborn factors, and in any event the group differences are slight compared with the individual differences within each group. Even if on the whole the higher grades contain a higher proportion of able individuals, that concentration of ability does not involve any loss of ability in the lower grades. There is no evidence whatever that the lower classes are being drained of able men. The social ladder is very narrow, only a relatively small proportion can rise, and the quality of the mass that remains is hardly affected by their transfer to another class. There is good reason for the view that the quality of the stock is remarkably constant, and that the proportions in which the factors determining it occur in the population are highly stable.[1] The biological theory of class and caste

[1] cf. Punnett, 'As a Biologist Sees It,' *Nineteenth Century*, 1925, p. 707.

is pure speculation, and its use in explaining the so-called decline of the civilizations of the past whose racial history and genetic constitutions are obscure is precarious to a degree.

(v) Social status is not in itself an index of good biological heredity. Wealth in particular cannot be closely correlated with inborn faculty in an economic system where ownership is highly centralized and inequalities are maintained by the laws of inheritance. In general, existing inequalities tend to perpetuate themselves, and the mass of the workers have to depend exclusively on the sale of their labour for their living, and have an income so small and a tenure so precarious as to make accumulation impossible and a change of status for themselves or for their children extremely difficult. In such conditions of highly restricted mobility and profound differences in the conditions and opportunities of life, it would be very surprising if there were any close relation between personal qualities and incomes.

(vi) Finally, a closer correspondence between status and inborn faculty would no doubt be brought about if interchange between social classes were more frequent, and individuals moved up and down the social scale more readily than they do now according to personal qualities. But on the whole the conditions making for greater social mobility would also make for greater equality in the distribution of wealth, and possibly reduce the differences of income to limits which are to-day compatible with membership of one social class. In such circumstances, however, birth limitation would probably be practised equally by all classes, and differential fertility, at any rate in so far as it is conditioned by deliberate restriction, would disappear. A social system based on justice and equity would from this point of view be the most eugenic of agencies.

There remains the problem of the definitely unfit, such

as the mentally defective. Here the eugenic case is at its strongest. Nevertheless it is necessary to keep a sense of proportion, and especially to clear both inquiry and discussion of policy from class bias and prejudice. There is no reliable information regarding the distribution of mental defect among social classes or occupations, though there is some reason for believing that there are considerable variations in its local distribution. The view that mental defectives are recruited largely from what has been called 'the social problem group' which is gaining currency in eugenic writings requires to be carefully scrutinized. It is based upon the finding of

Classification of Homes of Mental Defectives in the Investigated Areas. (Percentages).[1]

A. CHILDREN

Grade	Superior	Good	Average	Poor	Very Poor
Feeble-minded .	1·2	10·1	27·0	36·5	25·2
Imbeciles	5·9	23·7	36·2	19·5	14·7
Idiots	9·5	23·0	40·5	21·6	5·4
All Grades	2·4	13·2	29·3	32·7	22·3

B. ADULTS

Grade	Superior	Good	Average	Poor	Very Poor
Feeble-minded .	1·9	10·4	34·8	28·5	24·4
Imbeciles	6·8	19·9	49·2	17·4	6·8
Idiots	8·0	28·0	38·0	16·0	10·0
All Grades	2·9	12·6	37·2	26·3	21·0

1 'Report of the Mental Deficiency Committee' 1929, p. 202.

the recent investigations by the Mental Deficiency Committee,[1] which shows that feeble-mindedness is more likely to be found in slum districts in towns and in rural areas with a poor type of inhabitant.

A glance at the foregoing table, which I quote from the Report,[2] will show that the percentage of feeble-minded children who live in homes classed as very poor is not very different from that of children who live in average homes. It is true that the incidence in good, and superior homes is much smaller, but admittedly many of the homes were not visited, and the probability on the Report's own showing is that a good proportion of those not visited would be superior, good, or average homes.[3] It should also be remembered that in all probability many defectives living in superior homes did not come to the notice of the investigators at all, and so did not come within the scope of the inquiry. Moreover, the concentration of defectives in the poor homes is not proof that they constitute a genetic entity. Until the causes of mental defect are better known than they are, and it becomes possible to distinguish the hereditary from the non-hereditary types, it is reasonable to hold that the conditions of slum life in part caused the defects and not the defects the slum life. This suggestion is strengthened by the fact that the physical diseases which were found to be more frequent among the mentally defective children than among the general school population were just of the type which is associated with defective nutrition and an unhealthy environment generally.[4] It is possible that among the lowest ranks of the casuals and unemployables will be found many who are heritably defective. The State, in providing them with care and maintenance, is entitled to forbid them parenthood, and from this point of view the

[1] Report 1929.
[2] Part IV, p. 202. [3] cf. Report, p. 129. [4] Ibid., p. 83.

proposals made by eugenists for segregation or sterilization are deserving of serious consideration. But the treatment of the mentally defective is a question standing by itself. It has little bearing upon the larger issues of unemployment or the problems of taxation. We must above all avoid lumping together under the category of the 'unfit' or the 'less fit' all sorts of individuals whose hereditary defect is not established by direct evidence, but is inferred from their social or economic status. An example of such unwarranted procedure may be cited from the work of Major Leonard Darwin. He proposes that a list should be kept of all people in receipt of public assistance, including a record of the number of children in each family, and that all parents who had two or more children should be warned against having any more on pain of immediate cessation of assistance and of being subjected to inspection to ensure that the family was being properly cared for. If the warning is disregarded and the family found to be living an 'uncivilized life', then all its members should be segregated in some suitable institution. Public assistance is defined as including 'systematic in- or out-door poor relief, free feeding at school, unemployment doles, or insurance payments on account of ill-health'! [1] Whatever may be thought of such proposals on general grounds of social policy, it is safe to say that they find no support in genetics or in the psychological study of individual differences.

The chief conclusions which emerge from this discussion are briefly these:

(i) The legitimacy of eugenics as a scientific study is not disputed. There is need for dispassionate inquiry into the part played by inborn differences in determining social groupings and into the converse influence exercised by society upon the quality of the stock.

[1] *Eugenic Reform*, p. 385.

(ii) The relation between the inborn characteristics and their expression in actual social life is extremely subtle and complicated. The very same propensities may give rise to entirely different forms of outward behaviour in different social settings. Mental dispositions in particular are highly plastic and mental growth is socially conditioned throughout. The crude methods hitherto followed by the eugenists certainly do not enable us to so estimate the relative significance of environmental and genetic factors in social life. Those who have stressed the genetic element have been influenced not so much by direct evidence as by deductions from the theory of natural selection, assumed on *a priori* grounds to apply to the phenomena of social life. Theories have thus been devised to account for the rise and decay of civilizations in the absence of any real evidence of biological change, of the nature of the individual differences upon which the hypothetical selective agencies are supposed to have operated, or of the quantity of discriminative elimination. Such theories find but little support in history or sociology. The main factors of social change are social and not racial. Enormous changes can be effected in social structure and social life by methods independent of changes in the inherited endowment, and with a rapidity which finds no parallel in animal evolution. On the side of practical politics it is clear that the major problems of modern civilization do not depend for their solution upon the slow and tedious methods of selective breeding. They are essentially problems of organization, involving changes in institutions, knowledge and belief which have but little connexion with changes in germinal structure.

(iii) Once this is realized the claims of applied eugenics may be viewed in just proportion. Whenever there is evidence of serious hereditary defect, and when the defect cannot be extirpated save by the elimination of the stock carrying it, society may have the right and the duty to prohibit parenthood. Social policy must here wait upon advancing knowledge. Possibly in the case of certain types of feeble-mindedness our knowledge of its hereditary basis is already sufficiently advanced to justify immediate action in this direction. But the problems thus arising are not likely to be of wide scope, and their importance relative to the major issues of social reform must not be exaggerated. If eugenics is to progress farther it must free itself from the charge of class prejudice which it has too often invited, owing to its tendency to take relative poverty as a criterion of unfitness, and its readiness to provide pseudo-biological grounds for distinctions in wealth and power. There is in truth no real conflict between the demands of social justice and the requirements of biology. A social system based on ideals of equitable distribution would be the best remedy against the alleged evils of differential fertility, and every improvement in the ethical standards of society would reduce the discrepancy which at present exists between social position and personal worth.

INDEX

For Product Safety Concerns and Information please contact our EU representative GPSR@taylorandfrancis.com
Taylor & Francis Verlag GmbH, Kaufingerstraße 24, 80331 München, Germany

www.ingramcontent.com/pod-product-compliance
Lightning Source LLC
Chambersburg PA
CBHW062023270326
41929CB00014B/2292
* 9 7 8 1 0 3 2 7 6 4 6 6 5 *